Bears' Guide to the Best Computer Degrees by Distance Learning

John Bear, Ph.D.
Mariah Bear, M.A.
Larry McQueary

Additional writing and research by
Tom Head, M.A.

Ten Speed Press
Berkeley   Toronto

Other Degree.Net Books:
Bears' Guide to Earning Degrees by Distance Learning
Bears' Guide to the Best MBAs by Distance Learning
College Degrees by Mail and Internet

Degree.Net
A division of Ten Speed Press
P.O. Box 7123
Berkeley, California 94707
www.degree.net

Distributed in Australia by Simon & Schuster, in Canada by Ten Speed Press Canada, in New Zealand by Southern Publishers Group, in South Africa by Real Books, in Southeast Asia by Berkeley Books, and in the United Kingdom by Airlift Book Company.

Cover design by Cale Burr
Text design by Jeff Brandenburg (ImageComp) and Linda Davis (Star Type)

Disclaimer:
While the authors believe that the information in this book is correct as of the time of publication, it is possible we may have made errors, which we will correct at the first available opportunity. We, the publisher, are not responsible for any problems that may arise in readers' interactions with any schools described in the book.

Library of Congress Cataloging-in-Publication Data on file with publisher.

First printing this edition, 2001
Printed in Canada

1 2 3 4 5 6 7 8 9 10 — 05 04 03 02 01

Dedications

Larry's:
For Gina, Jesse, and Drew, who patiently allowed me to do this, and David Williams, my oldest and dearest friend.

Mariah's:
To Ada Byron, who made it all possible.

John's:
Can one dedicate a book to a co-author? Look, I've just done so. As Lord B was doubtless pleased and delighted by his eldest daughter Ada, so have I been by eldest daughter Mariah. We should all live long enough to be edited by our children. Thank you, Mariah, my little 'difference engine.'

Acknowledgments

We would like to thank Tom Head for the ton of research he put into this book, as well as his careful attention to detail, Jeff Brandenburg and Linda Davis for the sparkling design and typesetting, Joann Woy for the careful proofreading, Cale Burr for yet another in a series of fabulous covers, and Justin Wells, for being a one-man band: editor, project manager, parent, and in many ways, co-author.

Contents

Appendices

1. Introduction to Distance Learning: A 150-Year-Old Idea Whose Time Has Come

Distance learning has never been hotter. With whole degree programs offered over the Internet, courses on software, interactive CD-ROM, compressed video, and other great new technologies, the idea of earning a degree from the comfort of your own home seems utterly modern. Technology professionals in particular (a group you, the reader, either belong to now or will belong to soon!) are accustomed to receiving their information on the Net, getting training from a disk, interacting with colleagues through newsgroups, and problem-solving over long distances, sometimes without ever making face-to-face (F2F if you want to be annoying) contact.

Despite this modern buzz, distance learning actually has a long and distinguished history. In the early years of the 19th century, as the British empire was sending its politicians, bureaucrats, merchants, and others to the far corners of the world, the need arose for these people, now living in such remote places as Hong Kong, Johannesburg, and Chicago, to earn good British university degrees. The University of London was established to solve this problem, and it was based on quite a radical idea for the time: the notion that you could earn credit, certificates, and eventually degrees based on what you know, regardless of how you learned it. Then and now, many of the degrees of the University of London could be earned entirely by passing examinations.

In other words, if you know enough about calculus or C++ programming or business or marketing to pass an examination, you'll get the credit, and the degree, whether you gained your knowledge by sitting in classrooms for years, through training at a big corporation, or by apprenticing yourself to an expert.

This approach to education and certification arrived in America in time to benefit the likes of young Abraham Lincoln, who couldn't afford to "go away" to law school, but instead studied on his own, by firelight, until he had learned enough to pass the Illinois state Bar exam. The state of Illinois, thankfully, didn't care where he got his knowledge, as long as he could demonstrate it by passing their exam.

Distance learning grew slowly and steadily for decades, and then really took off in the 1970s, when entirely new nonresident universities were established, and some major state schools (like the University of Iowa and the University of Oklahoma) established distance-learning units within their schools. Now, at the beginning of the 21st century, it is truly possible to earn a bachelor's or a master's degree in almost any field of study without ever leaving home, except perhaps to take a local examination. This is a boon to working adults who want or need a degree for advancement, but just can't take the time off work.

One reason for the growth of distance learning in the information technology (IT) field is that it's increasingly true that a degree, particularly one in a specialized, competitive technical field, can be more useful than experience alone. You may be the best network manager, software engineer, or e-strategist in three counties, but all too often, if you don't have the right letters after your name, you may miss out on the better jobs and higher salaries that go to degree-holders, regardless of their competence.

But how useful are these degrees by distance learning? As long as they are earned from legitimate, properly accredited schools, they are at least as useful as the "old-fashioned" degrees earned by sitting in classrooms and lecture halls for years. Indeed, in one major study conducted by the National Institute of Education, many personnel and HR people said they preferred the degrees earned at a distance, in part because their employees took less time off work, and in part because such degrees demonstrate an admirable ability to work on one's own, without constant supervision. And now that Internet and other types of technology-based learning are an integrated part of virtually every tech company's training programs, distance degrees are practically mainstream. Graduates who, twenty years ago, might have balked at saying, "I got my degree by correspondence," are proud to say, "I earned my degree on the Internet." Same coursework, different world.

That phrase mentioned above, "properly accredited," is key, since there are not only a distressing number of fake schools (degree mills) around (as there have been for 600 years!), but also quite a few "gray area" schools that claim to be accredited, but, in fact, are accredited by agencies they started themselves, which are not recognized by the U.S. Department of Education or by the CHEA, the Council on Higher Education Accreditation.

Chapters 4 and 5 discuss accreditation in greater depth and tell you how to check out a school. With the ease of online advertising and cheap color printing, it has become all too common for sleazy schools to put up a great Web site, whip out some brochures, and make all sorts of claims. Many of the good schools, on the other hand, rarely advertise or promote themselves, either because they don't know how to do so effectively, or because they think it unseemly. And most of the bad schools—the illegal or barely legal diploma mills—advertise all the time, in major national newspapers and magazines. This book will help you separate fact from fiction.

Many readers will choose to deal only with the schools listed in this book. These listings may not represent every good distance IT program. Schools keep developing programs, and it is inevitable that more good ones will go online as this book goes to the printer.

In the next chapter, we'll discuss the range of undergraduate and graduate degrees described in this book, and then introduce you to this book's various helpful sections.

2. Computer Degrees and Distance Learning: What's in This Book

The fact that you've picked up this book suggests that you are aware of the growing impact of technology on your everyday life. No matter where you live, or what your current occupation, technology touches you: at the filling station pump, at the grocery store checkout counter, at the post office, at the doctor's office, and at your favorite fast food restaurant. Technology has moved from the world of academic research and the IT departments of large corporations into practically every facet of our lives.

But what does this have to do with computer and IT degrees? (We consider the terms "computer degree" and "IT degree" interchangeable here and throughout the rest of the book.) The relationship is this: This steady technology growth curve has to be sustained by skilled technology workers. These workers need to have the appropriate training, both academically and professionally, not only to innovate with new technology, but also to maintain and extend the vast number of high-tech products and systems that society depends upon today.

A recent study by the U.S. Department of Commerce suggests that between 1983 and 1998, the number of jobs in core IT occupations in the United States rose dramatically from 719,000 to 2,084,000. This increase represents a growth rate of nearly 200 percent, which is over six times the overall average job growth rate of 30.5 percent. The same report indicates that the high-tech job growth rate between 1995 and 1998 alone was 16.4 percent.

With this unprecedented job growth, as we mentioned above, comes constant demand for skilled workers to fill these positions. That demand translates to a world of opportunity for current and future IT workers. The greatest opportunity is really one of earning potential. A recent *Computerworld* article stated that the average entry-level application developer/programmer is commanding a salary of $45,000 to $60,000 per year, while software engineers are commanding $50,000 to $84,000 per year, and this doesn't even factor in company stock options and other profit-participation programs. These higher salaries are typically earned by those with more and better skills, education, and experience (though not necessarily in that order) in technical fields that are in high demand, such as electronic commerce and Web development.

Whether you are a working IT professional seeking to update your technical skills or change your specialization, or are currently working in an adjacent or nontechnical field, resigning your position to go back to school and be re-trained is probably not an option. The good news is that this book lists over 100 programs that can allow the working professional, as well as anyone who cannot attend traditional bricks-and-mortar colleges and universities, the opportunity to gain the critical skills and information necessary to take advantage of the world of high-tech opportunity that we've described.

Degree Options

In this book, we list IT degree programs not only in the traditional areas of study—computer science and information systems (more on this later)—but also in related technical specialization areas. While there are specific curriculum requirements recommended or required by various professional accrediting agencies (which will be discussed in chapter 5), the fact is that there are many very good nonstandard, specialized programs available from both U.S. and international schools that can qualify experienced professionals for higher-paying jobs.

Our criteria for including a school are as follows:

1. It offers an undergraduate, graduate, or advanced degree in computing, information technology, or a closely related technical management discipline.

2. The school is accredited, according to GAAP (Generally Accepted Accreditation Principles), or is a current candidate for regional accreditation. For a full discussion on accreditation, see chapter 5.

3. The degree can be earned either fully at a distance, with no visits to the school, or with relatively short residential sessions. Residency requirements are clearly spelled out in each school's listing.

As we noted in the introduction to this book, these listings represent the best schools that meet these criteria *to the best of our knowledge, at press time.* Distance learning is such a hot and growing field that good programs may very well debut the week this book hits the shelves. Mildly annoying, of course, but it's the way of the world.

If a program looks good and isn't listed in this book, we recommend that you check it out using the hints given in chapters 4 and 5. And please, let us know about any exciting new programs you come across. If we've heard about them, and there's a reason they're not in the book (i.e., the school is a clever phony, or we've heard other bad things about it), we'll email back and let you know (or write to you by mail, if you enclose a self-addressed, stamped envelope). If it's a new program, or one we overlooked, we'll write it up in the next edition, and in the meantime we'll post it on our Web site at *www.degree.net/updates/computerdegrees.* You can email us at *bcd@degree.net* or write to us at Best Computer Degrees, Degree.net, P.O. Box 7123, Berkeley CA 94707.

What's in This Book

Here's a quick point-by-point on the chapters that follow, why we included them, and what to expect.

Chapter 3: Choosing the Right Computing/IT Degree for You. Before you start investigating programs, you should know what you're looking for. Sounds easy, right? To guide you in this process, we describe the major types of computing/IT degrees and the type of job they qualify you for.

Chapter 4: Checking Out a School. We've said it before, we'll say it again: Deal with one of the schools in this book, and you won't be ripped off. But as there are so many other schools out there—some great, some quite nonwonderful—you need to know how to evaluate them. This chapter and the one following give you the tools you need.

Chapter 5: Accreditation. Perhaps the most important question you can ask is whether a school is accredited. Not all unaccredited schools are bad, and not all accredited schools are fabulous but, in general, you're safest dealing with a school that has GAAP accreditation. We'll tell you how to know for sure.

Chapter 6: Applying to a School. How many schools should you apply to? Must you have some prerequisite education? Do you have to take any entrance examinations? Should you invest in a counseling service to help you apply? These and other questions are answered.

Chapter 7: Alternative Ways of Earning Credit. Most technical degree programs have fairly rigid courses of study, but many do allow transfer credit, and some accept life-experience credits as well. This chapter briefly discusses these options.

Chapter 8: Distance-Learning Technologies Defined. What the heck is compressed video, anyway? How do online classes differ from discussion groups? Do I absolutely have to have a computer to take a distance-learning course? Basics of distance-learning technology explained in easy-to-understand language.

Chapter 9: Schools Offering IT and Computing Degrees by Distance Learning. The core of this book, this chapter profiles 100 institutions offering distance degrees in computer and technical fields, complete with contact information, Web sites, prerequisites, entrance requirements, and any special features we think you should know about.

Appendix A: Online and Correspondence Courses. There are many schools that offer distance-learning options for individual coursework, but not a complete degree program. In many cases, this coursework can be applied as transfer credit to some of the programs listed in chapter 9. Here we list 48 such schools.

Appendix B: For More Information on Schools in This Book

Appendix C: For More Information on Schools Not in This Book

Appendix D: For Personal Advice on Your Own Situation

Appendix E: Bending the Rules

Index of Concentrations and Specializations

3. Which IT/Computing Degree?

As we discussed in the previous chapter, there are a number of different specialization areas in the IT and computing disciplines. Which one is right for you? There are absolutely no right or wrong answers here. Each person is different, and each person's needs, both present and predictable future ones, are different. In this chapter, we describe the major categories of IT/computing degrees, and discuss the types of jobs that each may prepare you for. We have chosen these broad categories to contain all of the degree programs profiled in chapter 9. So, while a school may call its degree a "Bachelor of Science in Advanced Bit Twiddling," we submit that an inspection of the program's requirements will yield a fairly close match with one of the categories outlined below.

BSCS, or Equivalent?

At the undergraduate level, computer science is probably the most commonly sought IT/computing degree that there is. Sought, that is, by employers, if not degree-seekers themselves! If you've been seeking a job in an IT field and have perused the employment section of your newspaper lately, you have no doubt noted that practically every other job listing closes with the obligatory "BSCS/MSCS or equivalent required." That means they're looking for a candidate who holds a Bachelor or Master of Science in Computer Science or a closely related field.

But just what are the similar fields? Traditionally, for hiring purposes, these have been such fields as applied mathematics, electrical or mechanical engineering, computer engineering, or (in some cases) any of the "hard" sciences. More than anything else, they're seeking people with solid logic and problem-solving skills who have applied these skills in technological situations either academically or in the workplace.

The Good News and the Bad News

The bad news is that the Bachelor of Science in Computer Science is a rare find in the distance-learning world, particularly in the United States. The good news is that the field of degrees that are considered "equivalent" for hiring purposes seems to be widening, particularly for people with relevant work experience. There now exists an ever-widening variety of "hybrid" degrees, which blend business, applications, and computing theory, in varying proportion, into a single degree program. Some of these degrees will be described below.

The Degrees Described

Computer Science

Computer science is probably the most recognized computing degree, at least in the work force. Computer science deals with the theories of computing that underlie just about every specialization in the various IT professions. Everything from analysis of algorithms, to compiler theory, to computer architecture, operating systems theory, and applications programming is covered in the typical CS curriculum. If that sounds broad, it's because it is. CS graduates are generalists who are usually academically prepared for just about any computing position that may be thrown in their direction.

Prerequisites: At the undergraduate level, a strong aptitude for higher mathematics and hard science, as well as basic computer literacy, is generally required to be successful. Most undergraduate computer science programs require two to three semesters of calculus and linear algebra as part of their curriculum. At the graduate level, an undergraduate degree in mathematics, engineering, or any of the "hard sciences" is usually required or strongly recommended. At the doctorate level, it is presumed that you have a graduate degree in computer science or a closely related discipline.

Jobs: A degree in computer science, as noted above, prepares you for just about any entry-level position in computing. The most common titles these days are "Software Engineer" or "Member of Technical Staff," but in practice the positions could range from firmware programmer or compiler designer to application developer.

Computer Engineering

At one time, computer engineering was merely a subdiscipline of electrical engineering that specialized in the application of electrical engineering to the design of computer hardware and software. Sounds similar to computer science, doesn't it? Well, it is. In fact, we've seen computer engineering degrees that look more like computer science degrees than some computer science degrees! However, at their heart, computer engineering degrees are still focused on the design and construction of computers and computing devices. Computer engineers learn and employ many of the same skills as computer scientists and electrical engineers, but blend this knowledge in a way that enables them to build faster, smarter, and more efficient computer and networking hardware.

Prerequisites: At the undergraduate level, as with computer science, a strong aptitude for mathematics and science is a good predictor of success. At the graduate level, most programs require an undergraduate degree in electrical engineering, computer science, or computer engineering. At the doctoral level, graduate work in any of the aforementioned fields is generally required.

Jobs: A degree in computer engineering can prepare you for positions such as hardware designer, network engineer, and with the appropriate specialization, all the same jobs that a computer science degree prepares you for.

Business/Management Information Systems

(Note: Business/management information systems and computer information systems are commonly treated as separate programs in the field of computer degrees. However, the application of these terms can vary greatly from school to school, so look closely at a particular program's curriculum.)

Business information systems and management information systems, hereafter referred to as information systems, are strongly focused on the business applications of computing. Specifically, such programs address the analysis, design, and operation of hardware and software that supports management decision-making processes. Such information could include data pertaining to sales performance, employee utilization, parts inventory, or any measurable quantity of resources or output that can be factored into future plans or evaluation of current business performance.

Prerequisites: At the undergraduate level, no special knowledge is generally assumed. Many programs start out with basic college algebra and fundamental computing classes, building up to more advanced computing classes during the course of the program. At the graduate and doctorate levels, a business or computing background is assumed.

Jobs: A degree in information systems can prepare you for any number of positions in the business computing environment, such as systems analyst, data analyst, database administrator, and MIS specialist.

Computer Information Systems

While computer science, computer engineering, and even information systems are fairly standard and recognized majors, computer information systems is a relatively new hybrid discipline. Just as computer engineering blends elements of electrical engineering and computer science into a unified whole, computer information systems blends elements of computer science and information systems. CIS tends to be more technical than plain IS, yet far less theoretical and more application oriented than computer science. Most CIS programs include one or more high-level programming languages in their curriculum, as well as courses in networking, operating systems theory, computer architecture, and quantitative analysis.

Prerequisites: At the undergraduate level, a good foundation in mathematics, as well as above-average computer literacy, are highly recommended. Many undergraduate CIS programs require statistics and trigonometry or calculus as part of their curriculum. At the graduate and doctoral levels, prior work or academic credentials in any computing field are recommended, although some schools do not require this.

Jobs: CIS is the broadest degree, in terms of jobs it can prepare you for. Because the range of possible specializations within CIS is so wide, it is possible to construct a degree that would qualify you for many of the same positions that information systems and computer science do: application developer, database administrator, network security specialist, telecommunications specialist, and even software engineer, to name a few.

Software Engineering

Much like information systems, the term software engineering is used differently in different contexts. In days gone by, software engineering very broadly described the (sometimes ad hoc) practice of developing software for computers. Today, software engineering has become a very specialized area of computing that deals with the systematic application of engineering, quality assurance, and project management principles to the design and construction of software systems.

Prerequisites: At the undergraduate level, most software engineering programs we've seen are very similar to computer information systems programs, and have similar prerequisite recommendations. At the graduate level, most software engineering programs recommend or require an undergraduate degree in computer science or a similar field.

Jobs: As with computer information systems, there is a great deal of overlap in job qualifications. Graduates of software engineering programs are often found in the following positions: software engineer (of course!), application developer, and management positions such as software development manager or project manager.

General Studies

Several schools we've profiled offer a B.A. or B.S. in general studies. Some use different terms for these programs (like individualized studies), but the story is the same: They allow the student to construct (with faculty approval) a course of study that combines classes in one or more fields, but does not necessarily conform to any established curriculum or degree program that the school already provides. General studies programs are often offered specifically for returning adult students who may have acquired college credit in disparate academic areas throughout a lifetime of study, but have no way to apply them to existing programs. These are also known as "degree completion programs."

Needless to say, depending on one's prior academic experience and college credit, one could construct a general studies degree from coursework that closely resembles any of the degree programs we've already discussed.

Prerequisites: Program-dependent.

Jobs: Program-dependent.

Master of Business Administration (with IT emphasis) and Master of Technology Management

We couldn't resist mentioning the "Techno-MBA." Anyone who has worked in a computing profession in the last 10 to 20 years has heard that an MBA, when backed with a technical undergraduate degree, packs a powerful punch in the job market. The reasons for this should be somewhat apparent: Well-honed technical skills, when combined with strong business acumen and project management skills, can contribute directly to an organization's bottom line. This concept has become so popular, in fact, that in the last 10 years, many schools have introduced graduate/professional degrees that integrate the two concepts directly. These "Techno-MBAs," as they're often called, mix the traditional finance, accounting, marketing, and management curriculum with courses geared towards such areas as managing technical innovation, engineering management, software development management, e-business, telecommunications, and information technology.

The Master of Science in Technology Management is very similar to the standard Techno-MBA, but blends more of a standard graduate management curriculum with the same types of technical courses mentioned in the preceding paragraph.

Prerequisites: There don't seem to be many common prerequisites for these Techno-MBAs, other than those typical to most MBA programs, which generally only require an undergraduate degree from a school with recognized accreditation (more on this in chapter 5).

Jobs: Just about any technical management job, from development manager, to director of engineering, to chief technical officer. At this level, the jobs that are attainable by the degree holder are determined as much by real-life experience as they are by the type of degree.

In Summary

We've spent a good deal of space here describing the main categories of computing degrees and the types of jobs they prepare you for. Would you hate us if we told you that many of the jobs we've described are actually attainable in some cases by people with no degrees at all? One of your authors has worked with top-notch software developers whose degrees are in such diverse fields as English literature and forestry research. These comments should underscore for you that there are *no hard and fast rules that apply to everyone*. Just as there is overlap between some of the degree programs we've described, there is great overlap in the skills that they promote. To put it plainly, don't become too hung up on degree titles. While the computer science degree is popular, practically any up-to-date technical degree can net you a good position in IT. Choose the degree that best matches your technical aspirations, your capabilities, and other criteria that are important to you.

4. Checking Out a School

Two Problems, Two Questions to Ask

A degree program is, for many people, one of the most expensive and time-consuming things they will do in their lives. And yet some people will spend more time and energy choosing a refrigerator or a television set than they will selecting a school. For such people, one of two major problems may set in later:

Problem One: There Are Unpleasant Surprises Down the Road

Some people enroll in a good, legitimate school, but then discover that the program just doesn't suit their needs. We all throw around the term "IT" as if it meant one thing, but in fact, as you'll see in this book, information technology is a very wide and diverse field. IT professionals may work in a very people-centered realm, as network strategists do, or in relative isolation, as many Web developers do. Some spend their days with their hands on soldering irons and network cables; others in highly theoretical realms such as artificial intelligence or neural networks. Even a seemingly simple degree such as "computer science" may channel you more toward one or another realm of the enormous cyberworld.

So, you need to really make sure that the degree you're interested in takes you in the direction you want to go. If you're thinking of a specialization in "information science," be sure that it's as high tech as you think it will be, not just an old library science program spiffed up with some new servers. That is, unless your goal is to become a high-tech librarian!

Question One: Will It Meet My Needs?

You'd think people would learn this before spending thousands of dollars and years of their lives on a degree program. But we have received hundreds of letters from people who have had very unpleasant surprises after enrolling, or even after graduating. It is essential that you satisfy yourself that a given school will meet your needs before you spend any money. Make sure you know exactly what it will cost (no hidden "graduation fees," for instance), whether your employer will accept (and perhaps pay for) your degree, whether any relevant licensing agencies will accept the work, and so on. The checklist at the end of this chapter gives you some insight into how much you can find out online . . . the short answer is, a lot!

Problem Two: The School Turns Out to Be Less than Wonderful

Some people enroll in a distance-learning school that seems to suit their needs without looking at it very closely. And then, when they see their alma mater exposed on *60 Minutes* or *20/20,* they wail, "But I didn't know; they had such a lovely catalog." Now clearly, if you apply to one of the schools listed in this book, that won't be a problem. All of these schools have proper regional or national accreditation (see chapter 5 for an explanation of these terms). Still, it's our experience that some people will buy a book such as this, note all of the accredited schools, and still end up studying at a less-than-wonderful institution. Why? Well, maybe it was less expensive, or seemed easier to do, and it swore that it was just as good as the schools in this book.

In addition, there's the fact that good, accredited programs will almost certainly debut after this book does (distance learning being such an active, growing field). So, you may well be faced with advertisements or Web sites for interesting-looking IT programs that aren't listed here, and you need to know how to evaluate them.

Are they new, fabulous programs that came online after our researchers finished their work, or sleazy diploma mills waiting to rip you off?

Question Two: Is It a Good School?

If you have any doubts, concerns, worries, or hunches about any school, whether in this book or not, you have every right to check it out. It's a buyer's market.

You can ask the school any questions you want about accreditation, number of students, credentials of the people in charge, campus facilities (some schools with very impressive-looking catalogs are operated from mail-forwarding services), and so on. Of course, the school has the right not to answer, whereupon you have the right not to enroll.

For specifics on accreditation, including how to tell if a school is properly accredited, read the next chapter. For some basics on checking out a school on the Internet, read the next section.

Checking Out a School's Web Site

Keep in mind that a less-than-user-friendly Web site (more the rule than the exception) doesn't mean that a school is bad, or even that its computer science department is behind the times. Sometimes the natural bureaucracy of a big institution will result in ironies such as a major private school training some of the best Web technicians while their own site looks like your grandmother made it. Still, a really cheesy site is a warning sign, and it doesn't hurt to ask some questions about it. Don't be embarrassed to call the computer science department and say something like, "I'm thinking of attending your school, but I was sort of taken aback by the look and feel of your Web site." A legit school will have an answer (maybe the funding is tied up, maybe it was a student extra-credit project that got out of hand, who knows?). Then it's up to you to decide if these people are professional enough to do business with.

The Basics

No matter how well or poorly designed it is, just about every reputable college or university's Web site should give you at least these basics:

- Information about the college as a whole, and about the computer science (or other relevant) department in particular.

- Admission requirements.

- Exact degrees offered and their requirements, including course descriptions. Though this book lists much of that information, it does change, and the school's Web site will detail any new requirements or programs.

- A schedule of courses for at least the current and next term (semester or quarter), indicating course availability. Many schools will also list course availability for future terms. Since not every course is offered every term, this information can be very useful for determining how long it would take to complete your degree at a particular school.

- Application deadlines for admissions and financial aid.

- Tuition and fees.

Beyond the basics, other things that may or may not be available on a school's Web site include information on faculty and staff, facts and figures on the school or its programs, detailed information on financial aid or job placement programs, and links to other college resources. If you don't see these things on a school's site, email to ask. Maybe the links are non-intuitive or hard to find. If the information is not online, the admissions person or other official who reads your email may be able to get it for you or direct you to a place where you can find it. If they get enough of this sort of email, the school may consider improving its site!

Faculty and Staff Information

While not every school site has faculty information, those institutions that are most proud of star performers often do. Sometimes you'll even get the email addresses of key people whom you can query personally with further questions. Also look for:

- Faculty biographies and research publications (great for finding out if the people in your possible future department are specialists in the areas that most interest you).
- The chance to sign up for specialized information via an email newsletter ("For more information on our developing IT programs . . .").
- Names of student teachers and graduate students who can provide insider information.

Useful Facts and Figures

- Student-to-teacher ratio. Is one harried professor handling all the online students? Or is there a real dedicated distance-learning faculty?
- Estimates of non-tuition and fees-related expenses you can expect, including books, software, etc.
- Policies on transfer credits, life-experience learning, and credit by exams.

Information on Financial Aid and Job Placement

If you don't see what you're looking for, send an email. Maybe the "merit-based grants for minority students" page is about to go up!

- Non-school grants and fellowships of interest to IT students.
- Information on job-placement statistics. What percentage of graduates find jobs in IT right out of school? Does the school have an IT-savvy job-placement office? Does the computer science department have a special job-placement service, or are all students served by a one-size-fits-all career office? If the latter, what's the success rate in IT? Is it equally open to distance students as it is to residential folks?
- Does the department have programs to offer internships with top IT companies? What percentage of students participate in such programs?

Other Useful Links

Some school Web sites are really nothing more than "brochureware," but many can give you a solid sense of the institution and its offerings. Poke around as much as possible, check out student pages, read the school newspaper, and otherwise get what you can out of every site.

- Links to the school library and research facilities.
- Links to unofficial student home pages.
- Links to a CS or IT club or networking group for students.

- Accreditation info. As the next chapter details, accreditation is vitally important. Some totally legit schools don't mention their accreditation online, because they don't see the need. If you can't find a school's accreditation statement, however, it wouldn't hurt to check with the appropriate regional agency and just make sure the school is listed. The next chapter tells you how to do just that.

5. Accreditation: Why It's So Important

Many books and articles about choosing the right school say that the most important thing is to choose an accredited school. Unfortunately, some of these authors stop there, without making clear that there are many different kinds of accreditation, at least one of which is not only useless, but often worse than having no accreditation at all. Indeed, many less-than-wonderful schools (you won't find them in this book) start their own accrediting agencies, which are often just another button on their telephone, so that they can advertise that they are indeed accredited.

Regional Accreditation

In the United States, there are six regional accrediting agencies, each with jurisdiction for one region of the country: Western, Northwestern, Southern, New England, Middle States, and North Central. These accreditors deal with entire colleges or universities, not with individual departments such as computer science. So when, for instance, the North Central Association says that Bellevue University in Nebraska is accredited, that means that all of the schools, colleges, and departments within that university have regional accreditation. To find out whether a school has regional accreditation, contact the appropriate accreditor:

Middle States Association of Colleges and Schools
Commission on Higher Education
3624 Market Street
Philadelphia, PA 19104
Phone: (215) 662 5606
Fax: (215) 662 5501
Email: info@msache.org
Web site: www.msache.org
Responsible for schools located in Delaware, District of Columbia, Maryland, New Jersey, New York, Pennsylvania, Puerto Rico, and the U.S. Virgin Islands.

New England Association of Schools and Colleges
209 Burlington Road
Bedford, MA 01730-1433
Phone: (617) 271 0022
Fax: (617) 271 0950
Email: info@neasc.org
Web site: www.neasc.org
Responsible for schools located in Connecticut, Maine, Massachusetts, New Hampshire, Rhode Island, and Vermont.

North Central Association of Colleges and Schools
30 North La Salle Street, Suite 2400
Chicago, IL 60602
Phone: (312) 263 0456 • (800) 621 7440
Fax: (312) 263 7462
Email: info@ncacihe.org
Web site: www.ncacihe.org
Responsible for schools located in Arizona, Arkansas, Colorado, Illinois, Indiana, Iowa, Kansas, Michigan, Minnesota, Missouri, Nebraska, New Mexico, North Dakota, Ohio, Oklahoma, South Dakota, West Virginia, Wisconsin, and Wyoming.

Northwest Association of Schools and Colleges
11300 NE 33rd Place, Suite 120
Bellevue, WA 98004
Phone: (425) 827 2005
Fax: (425) 827 3395
Email: info@cocnasc.org
Web site: www.cocnasc.org
Responsible for schools located in Alaska, Idaho, Montana, Nevada, Oregon, Utah, and Washington.

Southern Association of Colleges and Schools
1866 Southern Lane
Decatur, GA 30033
Phone: (404) 679 4500 • (800) 248 7701
Fax: (404) 679 4558
Web site: www.sacs.org
Responsible for schools located in Alabama, Florida, Georgia, Kentucky, Louisiana, Mississippi, North Carolina, South Carolina, Tennessee, Texas, and Virginia.

Western Association of Schools and Colleges
985 Atlantic Avenue, Suite 100
Alameda, CA 94501
Phone: (510) 748 9001
Fax: (510) 748 9797
Email: wascsr@wascsenior.org
Web site: www.wascweb.org
Responsible for schools located in California, Hawaii, Guam, and the Trust Territory of the Pacific.

The Special Case of National Accreditation

One interesting accrediting agency is the Distance Education and Training Council: a legitimate, government-recognized agency that deals exclusively with schools that offer most or all of their programs through distance learning. While the DETC does have a totally valid purpose—many new distance schools are too innovative or unusual for the mainstream agencies—they have also granted accreditation to some schools whose programs are of questionable repute. This is a topic of hot debate in distance-learning circles, and the verdict is far from in, but generally speaking, DETC accreditation is viewed in the education world as less rigorous than traditional regional accreditation. This is not merely an academic debate, in either sense of the term. Quite a few regionally accredited schools will not accept DETC degrees for further education, and there are job descriptions and, particularly, corporate reimbursement plans that require a regionally accredited degree. Still, if you find an experimental new program on the Internet and want to give it a go, you should make sure that at the very least it has DETC approval.

Distance Education and Training Council
1601 18th Street NW
Washington, DC 20009
Phone: (202) 234 5100
Fax: (202) 332 1386
Email: detc@detc.org
Web site: www.detc.org

Professional Accreditation

Unlike regional or national accreditors, professional accrediting agencies represent a particular field of study, and therefore deal not with an entire college or university but with a particular department within that college or university. For instance, the American Psychology Association accredits programs offered by psychology departments.

For the fields of interest to this book—computing and engineering—the relevant professional agency is the Accreditation Board for Engineering and Technology (ABET). Professional accrediting agencies are operated privately, but must be recognized by either the U.S. Department of Education or the Council on Higher Education Accreditation (CHEA, an independent nongovernmental agency in Washington, DC), or both.

How important is professional accreditation? Not very, at least compared to regional accreditation, which is the principal measure of a degree's legitimacy in the worlds of academia and business. There are hundreds of great regionally accredited schools, including many of those listed in this book, whose computer science or engineering departments don't have professional accreditation. However, if you're torn between two programs and need a deciding factor, professional accreditation is as good a one as any. (Also, there are a few engineering graduate schools that require applicants to have earned an ABET-accredited undergraduate degree; more on this below.)

Accreditation Board for Engineering and Technology (ABET)

In years past, ABET focused almost exclusively on professional accreditation of traditional engineering programs, while a separate organization, the Computer Sciences Accreditation Board (CSAB), accredited programs in the computer sciences. In late 2000, ABET took over CSAB's duties and, to reflect its now-broader scope, has reorganized its accreditation function into three separate commissions. The Engineering Accreditation Commission (EAC) is responsible for accreditation of traditional engineering degree programs, the Technology Accreditation Commission (TAC) for engineering technology programs, and the Computing Accreditation Commission (CAC) for computer science programs.

A few things to note about ABET accreditation:

- Its focus is primarily on the undergraduate level; few if any graduate IT programs have professional accreditation from ABET.

- ABET accredits individual degree programs, not entire departments. Even very legitimate schools often blur this distinction, claiming on their Web sites that a department is "ABET accredited," when in fact only one of their degree programs has this award. For instance, Bruce Wayne University's B.S. in computer engineering offered at the school's Gotham campus could be ABET-accredited, while the same program at the stately Wayne campus might not be. It's not the engineering department itself that's accredited, only that particular degree in that particular field at that particular campus.

- ABET accreditation is more important in the traditional engineering field than it is in the computer sciences. Some graduate engineering programs will only consider applicants with an ABET-accredited undergraduate degree; in contrast, graduate programs in computer or information science have no such requirement.

- In the computer sciences, ABET currently accredits only residential degree programs that offer a broad general education in addition to the technical aspects of the computer science major. However, ABET has indicated that it plans to expand its scope in the long term, performing accreditation of more IT specializations. They have also acknowledged the eventual need for accreditation of nonresidential computer science and IT programs. More on this in our next edition, we hope!

- Shortly before this book went to press, ABET withdrew its petition for recognition by the U.S. Department of Education. The impact of this decision on how ABET accreditation is viewed within the academic community is yet to be seen. Our hunch is that there won't be much of a change; ABET is, in a very real sense, the "only game in town" for professional accreditation of engineering programs. For updates on this situation, please point your Web browser to *www.degree.net/updates/computerdegrees*.

Accreditation Board for Engineering and Technology, Inc. (ABET)
111 Market Place, Suite 1050
Baltimore, MD 21202
Phone: (410) 347 7700
Fax: (410) 625 2238
Email: accreditation@abet.org
Web site: www.abet.org

MBA Accreditors

Why list MBA accreditors in an IT book? For the simple reason that there's a lot of overlap between these fields right now. The tech MBA, focusing in a field such as e-commerce or systems management, is very hot, and a lot of management-oriented techies are hopping on board. (If you're *really* interested in business study, you might want to check out *Bears' Guide to the Best MBAs by Distance Learning*. Just a thought.)

For whatever reason, professional accreditation seems to matter more for business schools than it does in other fields. Again, it's hardly required, but corporate recruiters look with more favor on MBA degrees from professionally accredited schools, and this could give you an extra edge.

The most prestigious business-degree accreditor is the International Association for Management Education, formerly the American Assembly of Collegiate Schools of Business (and, confusingly, still referred to with the acronym AACSB). This organization is the U.S.'s oldest business-school accreditor, and the one that deals with such schools as Harvard, Yale, Stanford, and dozens of others. Smaller colleges and universities tend to deal with the Association of Collegiate Business Schools and Programs. The Accrediting Council for Independent Colleges and Schools works mainly with community colleges and vocational schools, but does accredit a small number of MBA-granting institutions.

The International Association for Management Education (AACSB)
600 Emerson Road, Suite 300
St. Louis, MO 63141
Phone: (314) 872 8481
Fax: (314) 872 8495
Email: webmaster@aacsb.edu
Web site: www.aacsb.edu

The Association of Collegiate Business Schools and Programs (ACBSP)
7007 College Boulevard, Suite 420
Overland Park, KS 66211
Phone: (913) 339 9356
Fax: (913) 339 6226
Email: acbsp@aol.com
Web site: www.acbsp.org

The Accrediting Council for Independent Colleges and Schools
750 First Street NE, Suite 980
Washington, DC 20002-4241
Phone: (202) 336 6780
Fax: (202) 482 2593
Email: acics@acics.org
Web site: www.acics.org

International Accreditation

Many less-than-wonderful schools claim to be "internationally accredited," typically by an agency with the words "International" or "World" or "Global" in the title. In the world of higher education, there is no recognized or accepted or useful concept of international accreditation. These so-called international accreditors may operate legally in their country, but it is safe to say that no university registrars, government agencies, and few if any corporate human resources professionals would accept their accreditation. There are, needless to say, no schools with "international" accreditation in this book.

No Accreditation at All

No new school is properly accredited when it opens for business. It typically takes several years of operation before one can apply to a recognized accrediting agency, and then the process may take anywhere from one to six years. So if a school states that it is not accredited, this is not necessarily a bad thing. It may be too new. Unfortunately, some bad schools explain to potential students that they are not accredited because they are too innovative, or too unusual for the recognized accreditors, or that because they are international in scope, they do not need to be regionally or nationally accredited. One should take such claims with a grain of salt.

The Bottom Line: GAAP, the Generally Accepted Accreditation Principles

Things are not nearly as complicated as they may appear from the above text, simply because there are plenty of distance-learning IT programs that meet the international standards of GAAP, or Generally Accepted Accreditation Principles (the acronym is, of course, borrowed from the world of accounting). These principles, which are acceptable to virtually every university registrar, corporate human resources department, and government agency, require that a school meet any *one* of the following six criteria:

1. Accredited by an accrediting agency recognized by the U.S. Department of Education.

2. Accredited by an accrediting agency recognized by the Council on Higher Education Accreditation (CHEA) in Washington, DC.

3. Listed in the *International Handbook of Universities* (a UNESCO publication).

4. Listed in the *Commonwealth Universities Yearbook*.

5. Listed in the *World Education Series*, published by PIER (Projects in International Education Research), a joint venture of the American Association of Collegiate Registrars and the Association of International Educators, with the participation of the College Board.

6. Listed in the *Countries Series*, published by NOOSR, the National Office for Overseas Skills Recognition, in Australia.

If any degree program fails to meet any of these six criteria, that does not necessarily mean it is bad or fake. But it does mean that the degree will not be regarded as accredited, and may well prove troublesome to the holder. With so many distance-learning tech programs that do meet the criteria of GAAP, including the 100 profiled in this book, why take a chance?

6. Applying to an IT Program

How Many Schools Should You Apply To?

There is no single answer to this question that is right for everyone. Each person will have to determine his or her own best answer. The decision should be based on the following four factors:

1. Likelihood of admission

Some schools are extremely competitive or popular and admit fewer than 10 percent of qualified applicants. Some have an "open admission" policy and admit literally everyone who applies. Most are somewhere in between.

If your goal is to be admitted to one of the highly competitive schools (such as Stanford or Carnegie Mellon), where your chances of being accepted are not high, then it is wise to apply to at least four or five schools that would be among your top choices and to at least one "safety valve," an easier one, in case all else fails.

If you are interested in one of the good, but not world-famous, nonresident programs, your chances for acceptance are probably better than nine in ten, so you might decide to apply to only one or, preferably, two, just in case.

2. Cost

There is a tremendous range of possible costs for the both undergraduate and graduate tech degrees. The least expensive program in this book costs under $10,000, the most expensive over $30,000. This is a case in which "you get what you pay for" really doesn't apply. The prestige of a top-name school may open a few more doors, but there's no stigma attached to a good degree from an accredited school, even if it's not the most expensive and/or most famous (not surprisingly, the two factors often go hand in hand).

3. What they offer you

Shopping around for a school is a little like shopping for a new car. Many schools either have perpetual money needs or operate as profit-making businesses. In either case, they are most eager to enroll new students. Thus it is not unreasonable to ask the schools what they can do for you. Let them know that you are a knowledgeable "shopper" and that you have read this book. Do they have courses or faculty advisors in your specific field? If not, will they get them for you? How much credit will they give for your existing credentials? How long will it take to earn the degree? Are there any scholarships or tuition reduction plans available? Does tuition have to be paid all at once, or can it be spread out over time? If factors like these are important to you, then it could pay to shop around for the best deal.

You might consider investigating at least two or three schools that appear somewhat similar because there will surely be differences.

Caution: Remember that academic quality and reputation are probably the most important factors—so don't let a small financial saving be a reason to switch from a good school to a less-than-good school. Again, all the schools in this book are good, reputable institutions, but there are many shady operators out there who are eager to offer you a deal, take your money, and then award you a worthless or even dangerous degree. That may sound alarmist, but we talk to people every day whose careers or academic studies have been damaged by a bad degree.

4. Your own time

Applying to a school can be a time-consuming process—and it costs money, too. Many schools have application fees ranging from $25 to $100. Some people get so carried away with the process of applying to school after school that they never get around to earning their degree!

Of course, once you have prepared a good and detailed resume, curriculum vitae, or life-experience portfolio, you can use it to apply to more than one school.

Another time factor is how much of a hurry you are in. If you apply to several schools at once, the chances are good that at least one will admit you, and you can begin work promptly. If you apply to only one, and it turns you down, or you experience long delays, then it can take a month or two—or more—to go through the admission process again elsewhere.

Speeding Up the Admission Process

The admission process at most traditional schools is very slow; most people apply nearly a year in advance and do not learn whether their application has been accepted for four to six months. The schools in this book vary immensely in their policies in this regard. Some will grant conditional acceptance within a few weeks after receiving the application. ("Conditional" means that they must later verify the prior learning experiences you claim.) Others take just as long as traditional programs.

The following three factors can result in a much faster admission process:

1. Selecting schools by admission policy

A school's admission policy should be stated in its catalog. Since you will find a range among schools of a few weeks to six months for a decision, the simple solution is to ask and then apply to schools with a fast procedure.

2. Asking for speedy decisions

Some schools have formal procedures whereby you can request an early decision on your acceptance. Others do the same thing informally for those who ask. In effect, this puts you at the top of the pile in the admission office, so you will have the decision in perhaps half the usual time. Other schools use what they call a "rolling admissions" procedure, which means, in effect, that each application is considered soon after it is received instead of being held several months and considered with a large batch of others.

3. Applying pressure

As previously indicated, many schools are eager to have new students. If you make it clear to a school that you are in a hurry and may consider going elsewhere if you don't hear from them promptly, they will usually speed up the process. It is not unreasonable to specify a timeframe. If, for instance, you are mailing in your application on September 1, you might enclose a note saying that you would like to have their decision mailed or phoned to you by October 1. (Some schools routinely telephone their acceptances, others do so if asked, some will only do so by collect call, and others will not, no matter what.)

How to Apply to a School

The basic procedure is essentially the same at all schools, traditional or nontraditional:

1. You write, telephone, or email for the school's catalog, prospectus, or other literature, and admission form.

2. You complete the admission form and return it to the school with the application fee, if any.

3. You complete any other requirements the school may have (exams, transcripts, letters of recommendation, etc.).

4. The school notifies you of its decision.

It is step three that can vary tremendously from school to school. At some schools, all that is required is the admission application. Others will require various entrance examinations to test your aptitude or knowledge level, transcripts, three or more letters of reference, a statement of financial condition, and possibly a personal interview, either on the campus or with a local representative in your area.

Luckily, the majority of schools in this book have relatively simple entrance requirements. All schools should tell you exactly what they expect you to do in order to apply. If it is not clear, ask. If the school does not supply prompt, helpful answers, then you probably don't want to deal with them anyway. Remember, it's a buyer's market.

It is advisable, in general, not to send a whole bunch of stuff to a school the very first time you write to them. A short note asking for their catalog should suffice. You may wish to indicate your field and degree goal ("I am interested in obtaining your B.S. in computer information systems through distance learning") in case they have different sets of literature for different programs. It probably can do no harm to mention that you are a reader of this book; it might get you slightly more prompt or more personal responses. (On the other hand, we have gotten more than a few grouchy letters from readers who say, "I told them I was a personal friend of yours, and it still took six months for an answer." Oh, dear. Well, if they hadn't said that, it might have been even longer. Or perhaps shorter. Who knows?)

The Matter of Entrance Examinations

Many nonresident programs do not require any entrance examinations, even at schools that do require exams for on-campus study. The main reason for this appears to be that nonresidential students do not contribute to overcrowding on the campus, so more of them can be admitted. A second reason is that nonresidential IT students tend to be more mature, and often have real-world work experience, which means that the schools acknowledge they have the ability to decide which program is best for them, and the savvy to do well.

There are, needless to say, exceptions. If you have particular feelings about examinations—positive or negative—you will be able to find schools that meet your requirements. Do not hesitate to ask any school about their exam requirements if they are not clear from the catalog.

Undergraduate Entrance Exams

Nobody likes exams. Well, okay, somebody out there probably does, but not anyone we want to meet anytime soon. The good news is that entrance exam scores are becoming less and less important to admissions committees. After years of evidence that scores are a useful, but not a vital, predictor of college success, schools are shifting their emphasis. Many now look more closely at an applicant's overall grades, the number of AP (advanced placement) courses they took in high school, their essays, their extracurricular activities, and all those things that say more about a person than a numerical score.

Indeed, some schools have dispensed with entrance exams altogether (Bowdoin College in Maine led the pack, all the way back in 1969). Still, even if a school doesn't require exams, it just makes sense to take them. High scores will still be impressive, and may balance out some other weaknesses in your application. And the top schools do still, in general, use test scores as a way of weeding through stacks and stacks of highly qualified applicants.

The tests you're likely to encounter are described in the following sections.

PSAT

Offered the junior year of high school, this test is not required anywhere, but it is a good idea to take it. Co-sponsored by the College Board and National Merit Scholarship Corporation, the PSAT tests critical reading, math problem-solving, and writing skills. It is very similar to the SAT I and SAT II and is a great way to practice for these key tests. In addition, a high score puts you in line for scholarships and other perks. The PSAT is administered by high schools; talk to a guidance counselor about how to sign up.

SAT I

Most traditional schools require the SAT I (usually just called "the SAT") for admission. Developed and distributed by the College Board (*www.collegeboard.com*), the SAT measures verbal and math ability. There are a wealth of test-prep software packages, books, and courses available to help you prepare. (Note that most nontraditional programs do not require adult students over the age of 25 to take the SAT.) Studies have found that preparation is important, but that you can get as much out of a $17.95 book as you can from a $900 test-prep course (and yes, the courses can be that expensive!). What it really comes down to is discipline—force yourself to spend a few hours a week with the book or the online program, and you'll likely do fine. A *U.S. News and World Report* article even suggested that superhigh scores can have a downside—students with perfect SAT scores and no extracurricular activities were seen as not well-rounded, and often rejected by admissions committees. Take that with a grain of salt of course—if you have perfect scores and a great transcript, the odds are low that anyone will hold a perfect score against you!

SAT II

These tests focus on a particular subject in a range of fields. You may want or need to take them in either of the math concentrations available; there is no computer- or technology-specific SAT II, though we guess that that will change over time.

ACT

Virtually all schools accept the ACT in place of the SAT I, though some express a preference for the SAT. The test is broken into sections focusing on English, reading, mathematics, and science reasoning. This last section is useful for future technology majors, and you may wish to take the ACT if only to convince a school of your aptitude for computer sciences, especially if your transcript isn't as strong as it could be in that area.

AP

Advanced Placement exams are an opportunity for high school students who've taken AP classes to demonstrate their abilities—and sometimes even get college credits, advanced college standing, or both with high scores. Different high schools offer different AP programs, but if you're lucky, you'll be able to take computer science and calculus. In the school listings, we note which colleges give credit for AP classes.

Graduate Entrance Exams

Just about every school listed in this book requires the general GRE (Graduate Record Examination) for admission to graduate programs; some require an advanced GRE as well. Good scores will help to make you more attractive to an admissions committee, especially if your background isn't as strong in technical fields as you might wish. If English is not your first language, most schools also require the TOEFL (Test of English as a Foreign Language).

Graduate Record Exam

The GRE is administered year-round at testing centers around the world. Check out the Web site at *www.gre.org* to find the center nearest you. Given on computer, the general test is divided into three parts: English, math, and logic. Even though the latter two categories may be more relevant for your career in computer science, you'll want to do well on all three parts, as many schools look at your aggregate score.

In addition to the general test, some graduate programs require that you take one or more GRE subject exams, in computer science, mathematics, and/or physics. It's up to you how much unrequired testing you want to subject yourself to, but if you're considering a degree in computer science, we recommend that you at least take the computer science test. It consists of about 70 questions specifically tailored to students who plan to seek a graduate degree in computer science, and it assumes that you've taken courses at least to the level of an undergraduate major in the field. If you've worked or studied extensively in IT-related areas, you should do fine even if your undergraduate degree was in something totally unrelated. The questions are classified approximately as follows: software systems and methodology (35%), computer organization and architecture (20%), theory (25%), mathematical background (15%), and advanced topics such as artificial intelligence, modeling, and simulation (5%).

The 66 questions of the mathematics subject exam focus on abstract algebra, linear algebra, and the ability to prove theorems and create counter examples (in contrast to the math section of the general GRE, which doesn't go beyond basic algebra). About a quarter of the questions require knowledge in other areas, such as complex analysis, topology, combinatorics, probability, statistics, number theory, and algorithmic processes. Many of these are skills you'll need in certain advanced computer fields, so you would be well advised to take the test if the programs you've targeted are math-heavy.

English-Language Examinations

The Test of English as a Foreign Language, or TOEFL, is often required for applicants whose first language is not English. The TOEFL tests one's ability to read and write English at the level of college instruction. Some schools specify a required score for those who have English as a second or other language; others just say "sufficient TOEFL score required." Usually, this means in the range of 500 to 600 points. Schools with "live" instructors (on CD-ROM, over television, etc.) may also require the TOEFL test that evaluates comprehension of spoken English. The test is given at testing sites in close to 200 countries, 12 times a year.

Test of English as a Foreign Language
P.O. Box 6151
Princeton, NJ 08541-6151
Phone: (609) 7717760
Email: toefl@ets.org
Web site: www.toefl.org

Exam Preparation

There are many excellent books available at most libraries and larger bookstores on how to prepare for the SAT, ACT, or GRE, complete with sample questions and answers. Also, the testing agencies themselves sell literature on their tests as well as copies of previous years' examinations.

The testing agencies used to deny vigorously that either cramming or coaching could affect one's scores. In the face of overwhelming evidence to the contrary, they no longer make those claims. Some coaching services have documented score increases of 25 to 30 percent. Check the Yellow Pages or the bulletin boards on high school or college campuses. You may well be able to find a local college or university extension program that provides good prep courses for a fraction of the fees charged by professional course providers. Expect to pay anywhere from $300 for a local college course to $1,000 for a professional course. The two main test preparation services are Kaplan and Princeton Review. Both also sell preparation books and software. To find out more about their services, go to *www.kaplan.com* or *www.review.com*.

Admissions Consultants

Some students seek help from professional admissions consultants, to write a cutting-edge entrance essay, learn tips for getting into the best programs, or otherwise get a foot in the door. These services can be quite expensive (from hundreds to thousands of dollars, depending on the service used), and are probably not necessary for distance-education students. If you desperately want to get into a top-notch program, and fear that you won't be able to present yourself to the best effect, and especially if you're investigating residential programs as well as distance options, such a consultant may give you an advantage. Only about 1 percent of students at residential programs have used such services, and probably even fewer distance enrollees. Still, if you're worried about your chances, and you are willing to spend a fair amount of money, you may want to check your local Yellow Pages or the Internet and find such a person. Do be sure to ask for (and check!) references, and/or check the person out with your local Better Business Bureau. The field is ripe for charlatans and well-meaning folks who just aren't as helpful as they could be. Be sure the consultant has experience with IT degrees, not just academia in general.

7. Alternative Ways of Earning Credit

Most IT programs have fairly rigid courses of study, but many do allow you to bring in some transfer credit, and some accept life-experience and/or exam credits as well. Each school listing tells what sort of credit the school allows, provided, of course, they gave us this information when we asked for it. Otherwise, if you have potentially applicable prior credits, or relevant life-experience learning, it never hurts to ask. Several schools, for instance, will waive courses if you have certifications or other professional credentials. So, while your MCSE certification may not technically grant you credits, it will allow you to skip one or more courses. That sort of thing. Here are some other ways you may be able to earn credits: exams, life experience, foreign academic experience, and correspondence courses.

Equivalency Exams

Equivalency exams are subject-specific tests that, based on your score, can earn you credits equivalent to having taken a college course. Usually, this is taken as equivalent to an undergraduate course, but there are graduate programs that will allow the credits as well.

Though equivalency exams are available in a wide variety of subjects, for some reason the IT field is poorly represented. Still, several of the schools listed in this book will accept equivalency exam credit toward the nontechnical requirements of an undergraduate degree.

The two major players in the world of equivalency exams are CLEP (the College-Level Examination Program) and Excelsior College Examinations. These tests are administered at hundreds of testing centers all over North America, and, by special arrangement, many of them can be administered almost anywhere in the world.

CLEP Exams

CLEP is offered by the College Entrance Examination Board, known as "the College Board" (45 Columbus Avenue, New York, NY 10023-6992; phone: (212) 713 8064; fax: (212) 713 8063; email: *clep@info.collegeboard.org;* Web site: *www.collegeboard.org/clep*). Military personnel who want to take CLEP exams should see their education officer or contact DANTES/CLEP at P.O. Box 6604, Princeton, NJ 08541; (609) 720 6740.

The exams are designed to correspond to typical one-semester or full-year introductory-level courses offered at a university, and they are titled accordingly. Test takers are given 90 minutes to answer multiple-choice questions at a computer terminal. Exams relevant to the IT field include:

- Calculus with Elementary Functions
- College Algebra
- College Algebra—Trigonometry
- Trigonometry
- Information Systems and Computer Applications

CLEP tests are given at more than 1,200 centers, most of them on college or university campuses. Each center sets its own schedule for frequency of testing, so it may pay to "shop around" for convenient dates.

Excelsior College Examinations

Excelsior College Examinations are developed by Excelsior College (Test Administration Office, 7 Columbia Circle, Albany, NY 12203-5159; (888) 723 9267; Web site: *www.excelsior.edu*). Formerly, these test were known as Regents College Examinations, and before that the Proficiency Examination Program, or PEP.

Though there are no Excelsior College Exams in any IT-specific fields, they can be used to get some of your "breadth" requirements in the humanities out of the way. While CLEP tests generally correspond to introductory-level college courses, Excelsior College Examinations are more geared toward the intermediate to advanced college level.

These exams are administered at Sylvan Technology Centers (*www.educate.com*) at more than 200 locations throughout the U.S. and Canada. Persons living more than 250 miles from a test center may make special arrangements for the test to be given nearer home.

How hard are these exams?

This is, of course, an extremely subjective question. However, we have heard from a great many readers who have attempted CLEP and Excelsior exams, and the most common response is "Gee, that was a lot easier than I had expected." This is especially true with more mature students. The tests are designed for 18- to 20-year-olds, and there appears to be a certain amount of factual knowledge, as well as experience in dealing with testing situations, that people acquire in ordinary life situations as they grow older.

Preparing (or cramming) for exams

Both testing agencies issue detailed syllabuses describing each test and the specific content area it covers. They both sell an "official study guide" that gives sample questions and answers from each examination. On its Web site, CLEP also offers practice tests with sample questions.

The testing agencies create their exam questions from college textbooks, so for studying they recommend that you go to the source. At the bookstore of a local college, browse the textbook selection for the course that corresponds to the test you'll be taking.

At least four educational publishers have produced series of books on how to prepare for such exams, often with full-length sample tests. These can be found in the education or reference section of any good bookstore or library.

Other Examinations

Here are some other examinations that can be used to earn substantial credit toward many nontraditional degree programs.

Graduate Record Examination

The GRE is administered by the Educational Testing Service (P.O. Box 6000, Princeton, NJ 08541; (609) 771 7670; email: *gre-info@ets.org*; Web site: *www.gre.org*). There is one general aptitude test and a series of advanced subject exams designed to test knowledge that would ordinarily be gained by a bachelor's degree holder in a given field. Subject tests relevant to the IT field include computer science and mathematics. Schools vary widely in how much credit, if any, they will give for each GRE.

DANTES

The Defense Activity for Non-Traditional Education Support, or DANTES (P.O. Box 6604, Princeton, NJ 08541; (609) 720 6740; *www.chauncey.com/dantes*), administers its own exams, as well as CLEP and Excelsior exams. Once given only to active military personnel, DANTES exams are now available to everyone. Tests include:

- Introduction to Computing
- Management Information Systems
- Fundamentals of College Algebra

How Life Experience Is Turned into Academic Credit

Many undergraduate distance-learning programs offer a great deal of credit for life-experience learning. Professional degrees, including many technical and computer-related degrees, tend to be less generous, as the course of study tends to be quite rigid and allows for less creative interpretation. Still, some schools do give life-experience credits for certifications. If you do hold a diploma or a professional certification in an IT field, it's certainly worth asking whether this will be worth any credits, and/or excuse you from any required courses. How do schools decide what's worth what? It isn't easy. Some schools and national organizations are striving toward the creation of extensive "menus" of nontraditional experiences so that anyone doing the same thing would get the same credit.

Credit for Foreign Academic Experience

There are many thousands of universities, colleges, technical schools, institutes, and vocational schools all over the world whose courses are at least the equivalent of work at American universities. In principle, most universities are willing to give credit for work done at schools in other countries, to the same degree that they are willing to accept transfer credits from American schools. (Please forgive us our provincial bias in this section. If you're interested in dealing with, say, an Australian school and have foreign credits, your best bet is to ask the school directly what you need to do in order to get those credits accepted.)

Can you imagine the task of an admissions officer faced with the student who presents an advanced diploma from the Wysza Szkola Inzynierska in Poland or the degree of Gakushi from the Matsuyama Shoka Daigaku in Japan? Are these equivalent to a high school diploma, a doctorate, or something in between?

Until 1974, the U.S. Office of Education offered the service of evaluating educational credentials earned outside the United States and translating them into approximately comparable levels of U.S. achievement. This service is no longer available from the government, which has chosen instead to recognize some private nonprofit organizations that perform the evaluation service.

These services are used mostly by the schools themselves to evaluate applicants from abroad or with foreign credentials, but individuals may deal with them directly.

The costs run from $50 to $200 or more, depending on the complexity of the evaluation. Some of the services are willing to deal with non-school-based experiential learning as well. The services operate quickly; less than two weeks for an evaluation is not unusual. While many schools will accept the recommendations of these services, others will not. Some schools do their own foreign evaluations.

It may be wise, therefore, to determine whether a school or schools in which you have interest will accept the recommendations of such services before you invest in them. As with everything else, shop around, and ask questions to make sure that what you're planning to do will suit your needs.

Typical reports from the services will give the exact U.S. equivalents of non-U.S. work, both in terms of semester units earned and of any degrees or certificates earned. For instance, they would report that the Japanese degree of Gakushi is almost exactly equivalent to the American bachelor's degree.

It is important to remember that these services are independent, unregulated, and often inconsistent. Work that one agency evaluates as master's level may be regarded as bachelor's level (or even less) by another. So if you feel one agency's evaluation is inappropriate, you may wish to try another.

Organizations performing these services include:

Educational Credential Evaluators, Inc.
P.O. Box 92970
Milwaukee, WI 53217
Phone: (414) 289 3400
Fax: (414) 289 3411
Email: eval@ece.org
Web site: www.ece.org

Education Evaluators International, Inc.
P.O. Box 5397
Los Alamitos, CA 90720
Phone: (562) 431 2187
Fax: (562) 493 5021
Email: garyeei@ix.netcom.com

Global Education Group
407 Lincoln Rd., Suite 2H
Miami Beach, FL 33139
Phone: (305) 534 8745
Fax: (305) 534 3487
Email: global@globaledu.com
Web site: www.globaledu.com

International Consultants of Delaware, Inc.
109 Barksdale Professional Center
Newark, DE 19711
Phone: (302) 737 8715
Fax: (302) 737 8756
Email: icd@icdel.com
Web site: www.icdel.com

International Credentialing Associates, Inc.
7245 Bryan Dairy Rd.
Largo, FL 33777
Phone: (727) 549 8555
Fax: (727) 549 8554
Email: info@icaworld.com
Web site: www.icaworld.com

International Education Research Foundation
P.O. Box 3665
Culver City, CA 90231-3655
Phone: (310) 258 9451
Fax: (310) 397 7686
Email: info@ierf.org
Web site: www.ierf.org

Joseph Silny & Associates, Inc.
P.O. Box 248233
Coral Gables, FL 33124
Phone: (305) 666 0233
Fax: (305) 666 4133
Email: info@jsilny.com
Web site: www.jsilny.com

World Education Services
P.O. Box 745
Old Chelsea Station
New York, NY 10013
Phone: (212) 966 6311 • (800) 937 3895
Fax: (212) 966 6395
Email: info@wes.org
Web site: www.wes.org

Correspondence Courses

Appendix A lists a number of schools offering undergraduate- and graduate-level correspondence courses in IT-related fields. This may be useful for a couple of reasons. First, some of the schools listed in this book allow students to transfer in prior credits; you may wish to take a few correspondence courses in computer programming or related fields before making the big jump to enrolling in a degree program. In addition, many graduate (and some undergraduate) IT programs assume a certain baseline knowledge of math and logic. You can fill in the gaps with correspondence courses, further ensuring your success when you begin your degree program. For details, including costs, delivery method (many courses are offered online these days, in addition to, or instead of, by traditional correspondence), and requirements, contact the schools directly.

8. Distance-Learning Technologies

When the first distance-learning degree programs debuted back in the 1800s, the technologies involved were pretty simple: pen, paper, and postal service. Maybe the occasional telegram if you were really high-tech. Now, of course, it's a whole different world. As an IT professional, or someone interested in the field, some of these technologies and terms may be old hat to you, but some of them are pretty education-specific, so it's worth giving this chapter a once-over.

A Few Common Terms Defined:

Traditional Texts: This means pretty much what it sounds like. While schools' definitions of "traditional" may vary, you can basically expect textbook, photocopied or specially printed readings, ring binders of assignments, and the like. A number of media may be combined—so you may, for instance, receive a textbook to study, but then get your assignments emailed to you.

Video Instruction: This can mean one of a number of things:

Televised instruction: Some local television channels, and one national cable network, offer courses accepted by a number of distance programs. (In some regions, universities broadcast classes over local cable access or public television stations. It's worth investigating whether this is an option in your area.) Knowledge TV, formerly Mind Extension University, is a national private cable system that offers instruction from regionally accredited universities. Subscribers can view courses at will, but to receive credit, they need to be enrolled in a degree program. Electronic University and Connected Education are two companies that manage course delivery with Knowledge TV, mailing out program materials, helping with registration, and so forth.

Videotape instruction: Many programs mail out videotapes to distance students; these are usually just tapes made of on-campus courses, which are sent out once the lecture is completed. Many distance students enjoy this delivery method for a number of reasons: it allows them to feel like they're part of a class, it structures the learning program with regular (usually weekly) deliveries, and it provides them with a library of tapes from which to review and revisit lecture material prior to exams or other assignments.

Compressed video transmissions: It is increasingly common for schools to beam satellite transmissions of lectures to remote locations—usually a corporation, military base, or cooperating university. Students then gather to view the lecture together, and perhaps have discussions or complete tasks as a group.

This was once a one-way street, much like a TV broadcast. Nowadays, some programs use videoconferencing systems that allow real-time interaction with faculty and on-campus students.

A number of corporate-supported programs now also receive what's called "compressed desktop video," which, as the name implies, can be viewed on a computer with a high-speed Internet connection. During these transmissions, students can ask questions online, interact with others, and otherwise participate.

Right now, these methods use technologies not available to the average home-based distance learner, and thus students have to gather at a site that has the needed equipment. As home computers improve and connection speeds get faster, the ideal is to have anyone be able to participate, from anywhere in the world. Stay tuned!

Online Instruction: Once again, this can mean a wide range of things. The ideal, rarely in place right now, but on the horizon, is a fully interactive Internet-based classroom, where students can take classes in real-time if they desire, or download them for more convenient viewing, interact with each other and with professors, download assignments, browse reference libraries, and take exams. Many schools offer a number of these services, and both the number of providers and usefulness of the technology are growing fast. Here are a few services and terms defined:

Virtual campus: This term means all sorts of things, and you really need to view the campus to know what a school offers. It may simply mean that the school's Internet site offers some basic student services—maybe the opportunity to register for classes and order course materials. Or, it may be a fully interactive site, with student support groups, ongoing Web-based classes, and more.

Virtual classroom: An Internet-based course delivery system, almost always presented in real time, usually text (rather than image) based, to allow for students with older, slower modems and computers.

Asynchronous: Used to describe Internet communications that do not require parties to participate at the same moment, or in "real-time." Email, newsgroups, and bulletin boards fall in this category. The advantage of these technologies for distance learning is that students can access information, join ongoing discussions, and exchange email with professors when and where they wish, a major plus for those with hectic work and family schedules, or who may live many time zones away from their schools.

Synchronous: More commonly called "live," or "real-time." In this mode of connection, students communicate online at the same time, as if they were in the same room together. This may be in a chat room, where brainstorming and discussion occurs, or, in some programs, in real-time online classes or electronic meetings with faculty.

What Methods Are Best for You?

There's really no simple answer. Some distance-learning students like the total independence of working when they like, contacting professors by voice- or email, touching base with others rarely or not at all. Others want or need the structure of weekly meetings, either at distance-learning sites or virtual gatherings on the Internet. As with any continuum, most probably prefer something in between and, indeed, that's what most programs offer. As you read through the listings in chapter 9, you'll find that there's a level of structure and interactivity for just about every need.

You are lucky to be working in a field at the cutting edge of technology. If any department at a school is likely to be really wired, it's the computer department, for obvious reasons, so even older, more traditional schools may have interesting things happening in their IT departments. If you don't see the level of connectivity or technology that you'd expect, ask! You have every right to expect your IT education to be as up-to-date and high-tech as possible, and if you're suspicious about a school's facilities, you need to investigate further. In the fast-paced world of IT, you simply can't afford anything less than a truly to-the-minute program.

9. Schools Offering Computer Degrees by Distance Learning

Information in this book, especially the school listings, changes fast: new names, new area codes, new degree programs, etc. We do our best to stay on top of things; updates and corrections are posted on our Web site at *www.degree.net/updates/computerdegrees*. But remember, our readers play a huge role in this ongoing process. Please, whether it's a defunct email address or a hot new distance-learning program, bring it to our attention at *bcd@degree.net* or *Bears' Guide*, P.O. Box 7123, Berkeley CA 94707.

People ask why we don't give tuition figures, and the answer is very simple: these things change so quickly that any information we print will be out of date by the time you buy the book, and will only end up annoying someone. Check out a school's Web site, or just call and talk to admissions counselors about costs. It really does pay to shop around, as costs vary greatly (as do admissions requirements, amount of work required, and just about any other variable you can imagine).

A Note on Degree Types

The number of schools offering degree programs in computer-related fields is fairly large, and the number of available degree programs is exponentially larger. Though every degree program listed on the next 100 pages is searchable in the subject index, we think many of you would rather browse this chapter listing by listing. To keep everything user-friendly, we've included a "Degrees offered" field that quickly summarizes the nonresidential (or low-residency) computer degrees offered by each school. Every degree program is classified as coursework-based, examination-based, publication-based, research-based, or template-based.

Coursework-based: Most of the degrees described in this book are earned by taking courses offered by the degree-granting school. In the United States, this is the traditional system: you take a class—say, Introduction to Computer Science I—pass it, get credit it for it, move on to the next. Once you take enough courses and amass enough credits, you get the degree. Of course, what makes the programs described in this book "nontraditional" is that the coursework can be done without sitting in a classroom. At the graduate level, many coursework-based master's programs and virtually all coursework-based doctorates culminate in a final thesis or applied project; when these are required or are recommended as an option by the school, we indicate as much in the brief degree description (for example, an M.S. requiring a thesis would be listed as "coursework-based/thesis required").

Examination-based: From some international schools (most notably the University of London), a degree can be earned by passing a series of examinations. The student is given a rough idea of what each exam will cover, and then prepares for the test on his or her own.

Publication-based: A (very) few recognized British and Australian schools (University of Luton; University of Technology, Sydney; et al) award Ph.D. degrees to those who have already made significant original contributions to their field. Some new work is usually required: most often a long paper synthesizing the candidate's previously published work. Schools generally print "by publication" on the diploma when the degree is earned through this method. When awarded, these degrees are meant to reflect a lifetime of dynamic and influential work; no reputable school awards these degrees lightly.

Research-based: This is the most common non-U.S. format for the Ph.D.; B.Phil. and M.Phil. programs also use this approach. The student completes an original and substantial research project under the guidance of a faculty tutor, and the degree is then approved by a committee.

Template-based: Largely a U.S. phenomenon, template-based programs allow students to earn credit by a variety of means (traditional coursework, equivalency examinations, life-experience evaluations, and so forth) and from a variety of sources (ACE-approved corporate training courses, military training, other regionally accredited schools, industry certifications, foreign schools, and so forth), then apply these variously derived credits towards a "template" set by the university for a given degree.

Athabasca University

1 University Drive
Athabasca, Alberta T9S 3A3
Canada

Accreditation: International (GAAP)
Year founded: 1970
Ownership: Nonprofit, independent
Phone: (780) 675 6100
Fax: (780) 675 6145
Email: auinfo@athabascau.ca
Web site: www.athabascau.ca
Degrees offered: Bachelor of Arts (B.A.) in information systems
(coursework-based)
Bachelor of Science (B.S.) in computing and information systems
(coursework-based)
Master of Business Administration (MBA), emphasis IT management
(coursework-based/project required)
Master of Science (M.S.) in information systems
(coursework-based/project required)

Athabasca University serves more than 20,000 students around the world through its distance-learning offerings, which may involve online study, correspondence, audio lectures, and videocassettes.

The B.A. in information systems is designed to be part of a double major, although it can be taken on its own as well. The 13 courses focus largely on databases, Windows business applications, and Java programming, with optional modules in topics such as C++ programming and artificial intelligence.

The B.S. in computing and information systems focuses somewhat more exclusively on software engineering (with Java remaining the programming language of choice) and databases. The program as a whole is also more formidable than the B.A. in the general areas of theoretical computer science and applied mathematics.

The MBA with emphasis in IT management is comprised of 14 courses (7 of them directly IT-related), two comprehensive examinations (one in general business administration and one in IT management), and a final project. Two residencies are required: a weekend session (which may be taken at any point during the program) and a residential elective course (which must be taken after the second comprehensive examination). The residential course meets in the evenings or on weekends, and may be completed at any of a variety of extension sites located throughout Canada and the United States.

An M.S. in information systems is under development, and will be available in September 2001. The program will involve eight courses and an appropriate applied final project.

Atlantic Union College

Adult Degree Program
338 Main Street
P.O. Box 1000
South Lancaster, MA 01561-1000

Accreditation:	Regional
Year founded:	1882
Ownership:	Nonprofit, church
Phone:	(978) 368 2300 • (800) 282 2030
Fax:	(978) 368 2514
Email:	adp@atlanticuc.edu
Web site:	www.atlanticuc.edu
Degrees offered:	Bachelor of Science (B.S.) in computer science (coursework-based)

Atlantic Union College offers nontraditional bachelor's programs to adults through its Adult Degree Program (ADP), which largely abandons the semester- or quarter-based course system in favor of a "unit" system; each unit takes roughly six months to complete and is considered equivalent to 16 semester hours. A unit course consists of intensive research projects, independent reading, and correspondence instruction. Two 9-day seminars on campus (one in January and one in July) are required each year.

The computer science major consists of two to four units of dedicated study in the field, one unit of humanities credit, one unit of mathematics and science credit, one unit of social sciences credit, one unit of religion credit, and elective credit as necessary to complete the program.

Students may also complete a special interdisciplinary major by studying computer science and a secondary applied field from among the following options: art, behavioral science, business, communications, education (with emphasis on preprimary or elementary education), history, interior design, modern languages (with emphasis on Spanish or French), personal ministries, philosophy, physical education, psychology, religion, theology, or women's studies.

Atlantic Union College is affiliated with the Seventh-Day Adventist Church, but students of other creeds are welcome.

Auburn University

Graduate Outreach Program
106 Hargis Hall
Auburn, AL 36849-5122

Accreditation:	Regional
Year founded:	1856
Ownership:	Nonprofit, state
Phone:	(334) 844 4700
Fax:	(334) 844 4348
Email:	gradadm@mail.auburn.edu
Web site:	www.auburn.edu
Degrees offered:	Master of Business Administration (MBA) in technical executive management (coursework-based)
	Master of Electrical Engineering (M.E.E.) in electrical and computer engineering (coursework-based)
	Master of Software Engineering (M.Sw.E.) (coursework-based/project required)

Auburn offers a number of master's degrees through its Graduate Outreach Program, whereby students complete their degree requirements at a distance (generally through videocourses, although a number of required courses are now offered online).

The Techno-EMBA involves a series of distance-learning courses that are organized around five 1-week residencies: four on campus at Auburn, and one final residency at Cranfield University in Bedfordshire, England.

The M.E.E. in electrical and computer engineering involves 30 hours of coursework organized around a student-defined, faculty-approved plan of study. All courses may be taken by distance learning, but students must pass a final comprehensive examination on campus at Auburn. No thesis or final project is required.

The M.Sw.E. involves 33 hours of coursework and, like the M.E.E., is organized around a student-defined, faculty-approved plan of study. All course requirements may be fulfilled by videocourses, and the final project need not be undertaken at Auburn; the only required residency is a one-hour oral defense of the project.

Ball State University

School of Continuing Education and Public Service
Muncie, IN 47306

Accreditation:	Regional
Year founded:	1965
Ownership:	Nonprofit, state
Phone:	(800) 872 0369
Email:	distance@bsu.edu
Web site:	www.bsu.edu/distance
Degrees offered:	Master of Science (M.S.) in computer science (coursework-based/thesis optional)

For years, Ball State University has offered an M.S. in computer science to Indiana residents through extension courses. It has now begun to adapt this very successful program to an Internet format. Most of the degree can already be completed through online study, and it is expected that the remaining few courses will soon be available in an online format.

This 33-semester-hour program is comprised of two components: a 15-hour core (computer science theory, software engineering, numerical analysis, and computer science research), and 18 hours of elective coursework (in a variety of fields, most of them theory-oriented). No thesis is required.

Bellevue University

1000 Galvin Road South
Bellevue, NE 68005-3098

Accreditation:	Regional
Year founded:	1966
Ownership:	Nonprofit, independent
Phone:	(402) 682 5069 • (800) 756 7920
Fax:	(402) 682 5091
Email:	online-u@scholars.bellevue.edu
Web site:	www.bellevue.edu
Degrees offered:	Bachelor of Science (B.S.) in business information systems (coursework-based/project required)
	Bachelor of Science (B.S.) in e-business (coursework-based/project required)
	Bachelor of Science (B.S.) in management information systems (coursework-based/project required)

Bellevue University offers several online business-oriented bachelor's completion programs in computer-related fields. Students enroll with 60 semester hours of previously earned credit, and complete the rest (including a 36-hour major) through online study.

The B.S. in business information systems focuses on basic computer systems theory, networking, Visual Basic, and Internet issues, and concludes with a capstone project.

The B.S. in e-business focuses on emerging technologies, computer security, Internet marketing, telecommunications, and Web development.

The B.S. in management information systems consists of a general 15-hour focus in management issues, a 15-hour focus in business information systems, and a 6-hour capstone project.

Caldwell College

External Degree Program
9 Ryerson Avenue
Caldwell, NJ 07006-6195

Accreditation:	Regional
Year founded:	1979
Ownership:	Nonprofit, church
Phone:	(973) 618 3385 • (888) 864 9518
Fax:	(973) 618 3660
Email:	agleason@caldwell.edu
Web site:	www.caldwell.edu/adult-ed
Degrees offered:	Bachelor of Science (B.S.) in computer information systems (coursework-based)

Caldwell College offers several innovative bachelor's programs designed for students age 23 or older. Courses are completed through a guided independent study arrangement; credit for prior learning is available through transfer credit, standardized examinations, and life-experience evaluation. The program requires one weekend per semester on campus.

The B.S. in computer information systems includes a 54-semester-hour major consisting of the following: a 15-semester-hour core in computer science (foundations of computer science, introduction to computer science I and II, systems analysis, and discrete mathematical structures), 30 hours in computer and business information systems (business spreadsheet applications, Java, Windows programming, accounting, statistics, microeconomics, finance, data management), and 9 hours of electives.

California State University—Chico

Center for Regional and Continuing Education
Chico, CA 95929-0250

Accreditation: Regional
Year founded: 1887
Ownership: Nonprofit, state
Phone: (916) 898 6105 • (800) 780 4837
Email: rce@csuchico.edu
Web site: www.rce.csuchico.edu
Degrees offered: Bachelor of Science (B.S.) in computer science
(coursework-based)
Master of Science (M.S.) in computer science
(coursework-based/thesis or project required)

Chico State offers B.S. and M.S. degrees in computer science by live satellite feed
to corporate subscribers, or by videocassette to individuals.

The B.S. completion program in computer science requires 128 semester hours of
coursework; 30–45 hours are earned through Chico, but the remaining credit must
be earned elsewhere. Transferred courses must fulfill very specific distribution
requirements. The 36-hour major is available with optional concentration in math
and science or in systems. Courses tend to focus on general computer science theory
and software engineering. As this is a ABET-accredited program, the mathematics
requirements are significant.

The M.S. in computer science involves 30 semester hours of general coursework,
a thesis or project, and a 15-hour concentration in one of the following fields: artificial intelligence and expert systems, computer architecture, computer theory, data
and file structures, graphics and image processing, operating systems and networks,
programming languages and theory, simulation and mathematical computation, or
software engineering and systems analysis. A maximum of 9 hours of credit may
be transferred in, but any transfer credit must fulfill the specific requirements of
the program.

Capella University

222 South Ninth Street, 20th Floor
Minneapolis, MN 55402-3389

Accreditation: Regional
Year founded: 1993
Ownership: Proprietary
Phone: (612) 339 8650 • (888) 227 3552
Fax: (612) 337 5396
Email: info@capella.edu
Web site: www.capellauniversity.edu
Degrees offered: Bachelor of Science (B.S.) in information technology
(coursework-based)

Capella University offers many programs with significant components in computer-related fields, including: an M.S. and Ph.D. in business with emphasis in communications technology, e-business, or information technology; an M.S. and Ph.D. in education with emphasis in online education; and an MBA with emphasis in e-business or information technology.

The online B.S. completion program in information technology requires students to hold 90 quarter hours (60 semester hours) of general credit from a regionally accredited institution. The last two years (96 quarter hours) are taught by Capella, and focus almost exclusively on the major, divided up as follows: 36 quarter hours of foundation courses (each addressing a major IT or IT-management issue in a survey fashion), 30 quarter hours of professional practice courses (in fields such as ethical and human factors of IT, communicating in the new media, system assurance, legal issues, object-oriented analysis, data warehousing, and complex adaptive systems), and an 18-quarter-hour concentration in e-business, project management, or Web application development.

Online certificate programs are also available in the following fields: e-business ventures, information systems quality assurance, Web application development, Web application project management, and Web application security.

Capitol College

11301 Springfield Road
Laurel, MD 20708

Accreditation:	Regional
Year founded:	1964
Ownership:	Nonprofit, independent
Phone:	(301) 369 2800 • (800) 950 1992
Email:	admissions@capitol-college.edu
Web site:	www.capitol-college.edu
Degrees offered:	Bachelor of Science (B.S.) in software and Internet applications (coursework-based)
	Master of Science (M.S.) in information and telecommunications systems management (coursework-based)
	Master of Science (M.S.) in electronic commerce management (coursework-based)

Capitol College offers several practical degree programs entirely through online study, with no residency required.

The B.S. in software and Internet applications encompasses a massive 69-semester-hour major (54 hours of software engineering and computing, 15 hours of tele-communications engineering), which includes courses in Java, VMRL, Web site administration, and Visual Basic, as well as a 9-hour block of coursework in C++ programming. Other required courses address such topics as network security, Unix, databases, and multimedia applications. Students are also required to undertake a special topics course and a semester-long senior project before graduating.

The M.S. in information and telecommunications systems management is a 36-semester-hour program organized around three 9-hour core components (human systems and decision science, information technology, and systems management) and a 9-semester-hour concentration (in acquisitions and project management, e-commerce, general systems management, or global telecommunications systems management).

The M.S. in electronic commerce management consists of 12 courses (36 semester hours) addressing a vast array of relevant management issues (including project management, strategic marketing, and research and development).

Each master's program may be completed entirely online, although it is possible to progress more quickly through the program by taking both online and residential intensive courses concurrently. Neither program requires a thesis or formal capstone project.

Carnegie Mellon University

School of Computer Science – ISRI
5000 Forbes Avenue
Pittsburgh, PA 15213-3891

Accreditation: Regional
Year founded: 1967
Ownership: Nonprofit, independent
Phone: (412) 268 1593
Fax: (412) 268 5413
Email: distance-info@cs.cmu.edu
Web site: www.distance.cmu.edu
Degrees offered: Master of Software Information Technology (M.S.I.T.)
(coursework-based/project required)

Carnegie Mellon's prestigious Software Engineering Institute (which can rightly be called the birthplace of software engineering as an academic discipline) now offers an online master's degree.

The Master of Software Information Technology has three phases: the core, the elective track, and the practicum. The core involves rigorous courses in the management, development, and maintenance of software systems; it ensures a well-rounded and useful curriculum. The elective track is available as a formal specialization (in real-time systems or software engineering management) or as a pure elective credit section where students are permitted to choose their own areas of specialization. Finally, there is the practicum: Students are expected to develop and manage a software engineering project in an industry setting and report on the results.

A five-course graduate certificate in software engineering is also available. The course addresses basic practical elements of software engineering in a concise manner, and looks as though it would be a perfect complement to a master's degree in another field.

The legendary Carnegie Mellon Master of Software Engineering (M.Sw.E.) itself is now available in an online cohort format; the prospective student must find a corporate sponsor and six other local students. Contact the school for details.

Central Queensland University

Distance and Flexible Learning Centre
Rockhampton, Queensland 4702
Australia

Accreditation:	International (GAAP)
Year founded:	1967
Phone:	+61 (7) 4930 9719
Fax:	+61 (7) 4930 9792
Email:	ddce-enquiries@cqu.edu.au
Web site:	www.ddce.cqu.edu.au
Degrees offered:	Bachelor of Informatics (coursework-based)

Degrees offered:
Bachelor of Informatics
(coursework-based)
Bachelor of Information Technology
(coursework-based)
Bachelor of Communication (B.Comm.) in multimedia
(coursework-based)
Master of Health Administration and Information Systems
(coursework-based/thesis optional)
Master of Information Systems
(coursework-based/thesis optional)
Doctor of Philosophy (Ph.D.) in computing
(research-based)

Central Queensland University offers a vast number of distance-learning programs, both by correspondence and online study.

The Bachelor of Informatics is a three- to six-year program incorporating study in higher level mathematics, business information systems, and one or more specializations in database administration, decision science, health informatics, information systems, intelligent systems, Internet technology, mathematical modeling, mathematical theory, multimedia studies, multimedia technology, software engineering, statistical modeling, or systems services.

The Bachelor of Information Technology also involves three to six years of work and focuses largely on business information systems, databases, software engineering, networking, and multimedia technology.

The Bachelor of Communication in multimedia addresses multimedia development, programming, business information systems, networking, and human-computer interaction. Students are required to complete a multimedia project before graduating.

The Master of Information Systems is a two- to three-year program focusing on databases, digital telecommunications, and information technology management. Elective courses are available in programming, networking, intelligent systems, and e-commerce.

The Ph.D. in computing generally takes three to five years to complete. The entire program is based around the student's dissertation (generally of about 100,000 words) and surrounding research.

Champlain College

163 South Willard Street
Burlington, VT 05402-0670

Accreditation:	Regional
Year founded:	1878
Ownership:	Nonprofit, independent
Phone:	(802) 860 2700 • (888) 570 5858
Email:	online@champlain.edu
Web site:	www.champlain.edu
Degrees offered:	Associate of Science (A.S.) in computer programming (coursework-based)
	Associate of Science (A.S.) in telecommunications (coursework-based)
	Associate of Science (A.S.) in Web site development and management (coursework-based)
	Bachelor of Science (B.S.) in computer information systems (coursework-based)

Champlain College offers programs in the above fields entirely through online, Web-based coursework. Students with fewer than 56 hours of transfer credit may elect to complete one of the associate's programs listed above, while students with 56 hours or more of transfer credit may proceed to the bachelor's program.

The A.S. in computer programming focuses on programming within a business setting. Students choose to focus (6 semester hours) on any two of the following: Java, C++, Visual Basic, or RPG/400. Other required courses address such topics as relational databases, software applications, and logic.

The A.S. in telecommunications focuses almost exclusively on computer-relevant telecommunications, with required courses in fast-packet technologies, network design, network architecture, and networking protocols.

The A.S. in Web site development and management addresses HTML scripting, e-commerce, relational databases, and software applications.

The B.S. in computer information systems is available with optional tracks emphasizing computer programming, telecommunications, or Web site development and management, as per above.

Charles Sturt University

Locked Bag 676
Wagga Wagga, NSW 2678
Australia

Accreditation:	International (GAAP)
Year founded:	1989
Ownership:	Nonprofit
Phone:	+61 (2) 6933 2666
Fax:	+61 (2) 6933 2799
Email:	inquiry@csu.edu.au
Web site:	www.csu.edu.au
Degrees offered:	Bachelor of Applied Science (B.A.S.) in information technology (coursework-based)
	Bachelor of Spatial Information Systems (coursework-based)
	Master of Information Technology (coursework-based/project optional)
	Doctor of Philosophy (Ph.D.) in environmental and information science (research-based)
	Doctor of Philosophy (Ph.D.) in information studies (research-based)
	Doctor of Philosophy (Ph.D.) in information technology (research-based)

As the largest distance education provider in Australia, Charles Sturt University offers courses online and by correspondence to students worldwide.

The Bachelor of Applied Science (B.A.S.) in information technology consists of 24 modules and generally takes four to six years to complete. Concentration options include biocomputing and complexity, data analysis, distributed systems, e-commerce, environment and resources, geographic information systems and remote sensing, intelligent systems, Internet publishing, and multimedia and visualization. Life-experience and transfer credit can be applied to the degree.

The Bachelor of Spatial Information Systems also consists of 24 modules. Students may opt to undertake an 8-module specialization in information technology, marketing and management, spatial technology, statistics, or urban environment.

The Master of Information Technology is a highly flexible program based on 10 graduate-level modules and generally takes about two years to complete. Coursework covers applied neural networks, artificial intelligence, comparative information modeling, concurrent programming, e-commerce, evolutionary and adaptive robotics, machine learning, machine vision systems, object-oriented programming and systems modeling, and strategic information management. No thesis is required, although students may elect to undertake an independent project.

The Ph.D. normally takes four to six years of research and consists almost exclusively of the student's dissertation (generally of about 100,000 words).

Charter Oak State College

55 Paul J. Manafort Drive
New Britain, CT 06053-2142

Accreditation:	Regional
Year founded:	1973
Ownership:	Nonprofit, state
Phone:	(860) 832 3855
Fax:	(860) 832 3999
Email:	info@cosc.edu
Web site:	www.cosc.edu
Degrees offered:	B.A. or B.S. in general studies (computer science studies) (template-based)
	B.A. or B.S. in general studies (individualized) (template-based)
	B.A. or B.S. in general studies (information systems) (template-based)

This college is operated by the Connecticut Board for State Academic Awards and offers the Bachelor of Arts and Bachelor of Science in general studies. Students may construct an individualized program of study in an interdisciplinary field (with faculty approval), or choose to follow one (or more) of the 40 curricular concentration models already available, including computer science studies and information systems.

Each student is responsible for amassing a minimum of 120 semester hours, which may come from COSC's own courses (correspondence, online, or video-based), equivalency examinations, military study, portfolio assessment, or courses taken at other regionally accredited institutions. The degree requires that at least half the credits be in the arts and sciences. Only students residing in the United States may enroll.

The focus in computer science studies primarily emphasizes theoretical computer science, applied mathematics, and databases; software engineering and networking are also addressed. The information systems emphasis deals with statistics, logic, databases, and business information systems. For either concentration, up to 24 semester hours of credit can be earned through the subject GRE examination in computer science.

City University

335 116th Avenue Southeast
Bellevue, WA 98004

Accreditation: Regional
Year founded: 1973
Ownership: Nonprofit, independent
Phone: (425) 637 1010 • (800) 426 5596
Fax: (425) 277 2437
Email: info@cityu.edu
Web site: www.cityu.edu
Degrees offered: Bachelor of Science (B.S.) in computer systems
(coursework-based)
Bachelor of Science (B.S.) in e-commerce
(coursework-based)
Master of Science (M.S.) in computer systems
(coursework-based/project required)

City University offers many distance-learning programs entirely through online study or through more traditional means.

The B.S. in computer systems is a 180-quarter-hour (120-semester-hour) program, half devoted to general distribution requirements and the other half to the major. The major is comprised of 65 quarter hours of coursework (focusing on software applications, business information systems, and software engineering) and a 25-quarter-hour specialization in computer programming, Internetworking, networking and telecommunications, networking technologies, or an individualized faculty-approved field of study.

The B.S. in e-commerce involves a 90-quarter-hour general major (addressing both business and computer issues), including a 25-quarter-hour e-commerce specialization (addressing such issues as Internet marketing, Web publishing, computer security, and international business).

The M.S. in computer systems involves 45 quarter hours of study, which must include a 3-hour applied research project. Coursework focuses on business information systems, software engineering, and networking.

An online MBA specializing in information systems is also available.

Colorado State University

Division of Educational Outreach
Spruce Hall
Fort Collins, CO 80523-1040

Accreditation:	Regional
Year founded:	1870
Ownership:	Nonprofit, state
Phone:	(970) 491 5288 • (800) 525 4950
Fax:	(970) 491 7885
Email:	questions@learn.colostate.edu
Web site:	www.colostate.edu
Degrees offered:	Master of Science (M.S.) in computer science (coursework-based/thesis optional)

Colorado State University's Network for Learning (CSUN) offers master's degrees in several fields through videocourses, and many courses are now available through online study as well.

The 39-semester-hour M.S. in computer science involves 13 courses (or 11 courses and a thesis) on a variety of computer science–related subjects organized around a student-defined, faculty-approved program of study and based on available courses (in fields such as artificial intelligence, software engineering, databases, computer architecture, and networking). Students who elect not to undertake the thesis must complete a short research paper.

At one time Colorado State University offered an online second bachelor's program in computer science for students who hold degrees in another field; while this program is not accepting new applicants at the present time, it may reopen later. Contact the school for details.

The following certificates can also be completed by distance learning (generally through online study alone): AMADEUS reservation computer system, APOLLO reservation computer system, cyber travel specialist, SABRE reservation computer system, and WORLDSPAN reservation computer system.

Columbia Union College

External Degree Program
7600 Flower Avenue
Wilkinson Hall, Room 336A
Takoma Park, MD 20912-7796

Accreditation: Regional
Year founded: 1904
Ownership: Nonprofit, church
Phone: (301) 891 4124 • (800) 835 4212
Email: hsi@cuc.edu
Web site: www.cuc.edu
Degrees offered: Bachelor of Science (B.S.) in information systems
(coursework-based/template-based)

Columbia Union College offers a B.S. degree program in information systems
entirely through distance-learning methods with no on-campus attendance
required.

The program itself focuses largely on system administration issues as relevant to a
business setting. While the curriculum is without question business-oriented (with
courses in fields such as management information systems and project management), the more traditionally computer-related courses (in Unix administration,
C++ programming, computer security, and other issues) suggest a rigorous and
highly practical program.

Although much of the instruction will take place through correspondence and
online study, credit for prior coursework, examinations, and life experience may
be awarded after the student has enrolled and completed 24 hours of coursework
through Columbia Union College. The program concludes with an extensive
student research project, which normally takes at least two semesters to complete.

Columbia Union College is affiliated with the Seventh-Day Adventist Church,
but students of other creeds are welcome.

Columbus State University

4225 University Avenue
Columbus, GA 31907-5645

Accreditation:	Regional
Year founded:	1958
Ownership:	Nonprofit, state
Phone:	(706) 568 2035
Fax:	(706) 568 2123
Email:	inquiry@csuonline.edu
Web site:	www.csuonline.edu
Degrees offered:	Master of Science (M.S.) in applied computer science (coursework-based)

Columbus State University offers an M.S. in applied computer science entirely through online study and proctored examinations; the program is intended primarily for software professionals. Twelve courses (36 semester hours) are required for graduation. The eight core courses address client-server database systems, Web site development, software architecture, networking, and GUI development; the four elective courses may be taken in almost any field on an as-available basis. No thesis is required.

Curtin University of Technology

G.P.O. Box U 1987
Perth, Western Australia 6845
Australia

Accreditation:	International (GAAP)
Year founded:	1967
Ownership:	Nonprofit, independent
Phone:	+61 (8) 9266 9266
Email:	customer-service@curtin.edu.au
Web site:	www.curtin.edu.au
Degrees offered:	Master of Applied Science in information management (coursework-based/project required)
	Master of Philosophy (M.Phil.) in Internet studies (research-based)
	Doctor of Philosophy (Ph.D.) in Internet studies (research-based)

Curtin University of Technology offers quite a few degrees by distance learning. Students are given a study packet at the beginning of each semester that consists of a course plan, study guide, a reader, and other appropriate supplemental information (audiotapes, videocassettes, slides or photographs, maps or charts, and disks or CD-ROMs). Many courses may also be completed through online study.

The Master of Applied Science in information management is available with specialization in information and library studies or records management and archives. Each track consists of 11 modules and requires a capstone project.

The M.Phil. and Ph.D. programs in Internet studies deal with interdisciplinary issues related to the Internet: online ethics, Internet-rendered art, Internet music, Internet interpersonal communications, cyber religions, and so forth. The Ph.D. thesis generally runs to about 100,000 words and takes four to six years to complete; the M.Phil. thesis is substantially shorter and generally runs two to three years.

Deakin University

Deakin International
336 Glenferrie Road
Malvern, Victoria 3144
Australia

Accreditation:	International (GAAP)
Year founded:	1974
Ownership:	Nonprofit
Phone:	+61 (3) 9244 5095
Fax:	+61 (3) 9244 5094
Web site:	www.deakin.edu.au
Degrees offered:	Master of Commerce (M.Com.) in management information systems (coursework-based)

Top-rated Deakin University offers distance-learning programs to students worldwide through Deakin International, the overseas student office. Most instruction takes place online or through correspondence, although the majority of courses also require proctored examinations.

The M.Com. in management information systems consists of three core competencies (accounting, economics, and business information systems) and a specialization in management information systems. As such, fully half of the degree requirements focus solely on business-related computing. No thesis or project is required. This program generally takes about two years to complete externally.

Drexel University

3141 Chestnut Street
Philadelphia, PA 19104

Accreditation:	Regional
Year founded:	1891
Ownership:	Nonprofit, independent
Phone:	(215) 895 2000 • (800) 237 3935
Fax:	(215) 895 1414
Email:	admissions@drexel.edu
Web site:	www.drexel.edu
Degrees offered:	Master of Science (M.S.) in information systems (coursework-based)
	Master of Science (M.S.) in library science with emphasis in management of digital information (coursework-based)

Drexel University offers several master's degree programs online: the M.S. in information systems, an M.S. in library science with emphasis in management of digital information, and a "Techno-MBA" that can be completed through a mix of online study and short residency sessions.

The M.S. in information systems involves 60 quarter hours (40 semester hours) of coursework: 32 quarter hours of required courses (addressing subjects such as database management, human-computer interaction, distributed computing, and software project management), 16 quarter hours of electives (chosen from a long list of fields including knowledge-based systems, language processing, content representation, visual information retrieval, and computer-supported cooperative work), and 12 quarter hours of courses in interdisciplinary work (such as bioinformatics, cognitive psychology, software documentation, or telecommunications policy).

The M.S. in library and information science with emphasis in management of digital information focuses largely on computer-related issues; library and information science issues are addressed, but they're secondary to the primary curriculum (which addresses such issues as Internet information resource design, content representation, human-computer interaction, action research, and management of information organizations).

East Carolina University

School of Industry and Technology
120 Rawl
Greenville, NC 27858-4353

Accreditation:	Regional
Year founded:	1907
Ownership:	Nonprofit, state
Phone:	(252) 328 6704
Web site:	www.sit.ecu.edu
Degrees offered:	Master of Science (M.S.) in industrial technology, emphasis on digital communications (coursework-based/research project required)

East Carolina University offers an M.S. in industrial technology with emphasis in digital communications entirely through online study. Students complete 36 semester hours of work: 15 hours of core courses in industrial technology (including courses on Internet research methods and technical presentations), 18 hours of courses in digital communications (including courses on computer networking hardware, networking technology, and technology assessment), and a 3-hour research project.

Edith Cowan University

International Students Office
Claremont, Western Australia 6010
Australia

Accreditation:	International (GAAP)
Year founded:	1990
Ownership:	Nonprofit, state
Phone:	+61 (9) 273 8681
Email:	extstudi@echidna.cowan.edu.au
Web site:	www.cowan.edu.au
Degrees offered:	Bachelor of Business (B.Bus.) in information systems (coursework-based)
	Master of Science (M.S.) in information science (coursework-based/thesis or project required)

This school (formerly known as Western Australian College of Advanced Education) offers a number of interesting programs entirely through distance education. Distance-learning methods employed may include workbooks and/or study guides, additional reading, audio-visual materials, online study, and other instructional media. In addition, students may be directed to obtain and read various necessary texts and journal articles.

The B.Bus. in information systems consists of 24 modules: 8 core modules in business and management, 8 specialization modules in information systems (heavily stressing software engineering, databases, and networking), and 8 elective modules in a related field of the student's choice (which means that 2/3 of the program can be exclusively computer-related if the student so chooses).

The M.S. in information science is available with two tracks: interactive information technology and information retrieval, or specialized information services. The program consists of 6 academic modules, 2 research preparation modules, and a thesis or project; average duration is two years.

Empire State College

Center for Distance Learning
3 Union Avenue
Saratoga Springs, NY 12866-4391

Accreditation:	Regional
Year founded:	1971
Ownership:	Nonprofit, state
Phone:	(518) 587 2100 • (800) 847 3000
Fax:	(518) 587 2660
Email:	cdl@esc.edu
Web site:	www.esc.edu
Degrees offered:	Bachelor of Arts (B.A.) or Bachelor of Science (B.S.) with an individualized concentration (template-based)

A part of the State University of New York (SUNY) system, Empire State College has been a longtime leader in individualized academic programs. Its bachelor's degrees require no on-campus residency. Credit may come from Empire State's own distance courses, through standardized examinations, through transfer credit, through life-experience evaluation, or through on-campus courses offered at 40 locations throughout the state of New York.

Students begin by defining a plan of study; the concentration (effectively a major, although it doesn't appear on the diploma) can be in a computer-related field (computer information systems, Internet studies, software engineering) or in virtually any interdisciplinary field (cognitive science, management information systems, human-computer interaction).

Excelsior College

7 Columbia Circle
Albany, NY 12203-5159

Accreditation: Regional
Year founded: 1971
Ownership: Nonprofit, independent
Phone: (518) 464 8500 • (888) 647 2388
Fax: (518) 464 8777
Email: admissions@excelsior.edu
Web site: www.excelsior.edu
Degrees offered: Associate of Science (A.S.) in computer software
(template-based)
Bachelor of Science (B.S.) in computer information systems
(template-based)
Bachelor of Science (B.S.) in computer technology
(template-based)

Excelsior College (formerly known as Regents College) is the largest nonresident degree program in the United States. Rather than following a coursework-based model, Excelsior permits students to fulfill specific degree requirements though any of a variety of means: transfer credit from other regionally accredited schools, standardized examinations, military training, ACE-approved professional training, and certifications (ICCP, Novell, and others, especially for the B.S. in computer information systems; see below). Excelsior also offers its own brand of standardized examinations (Excelsior College Examinations or ECEs).

The A.S. in computer science is a 60-semester-hour program with a 30-hour major; students must fulfill specific core credit requirements in four fields (basic computing, computer architecture or Assembly language, data structures or telecommunications, and systems analysis) and complete 18 hours of relevant field electives.

The B.S. in computer information systems is a highly innovative program designed specifically for IT professionals. The MCSE, MCP, and Comp TIA examinations can be turned into significant credit and applied towards the degree. Students may also take advantage of the other nontraditional credit options described above. (See *www.itdegree.com* for specifics on this program.)

The B.S. in computer technology involves a 48-hour major (of which at least 16 hours must be upper-level) consisting of 30 hours of core credit distribution requirements (in circuit theory, computer architecture, electronics, digital electronics, microprocessors, electronic communications, and computer programming) and 18 hours of electives. This program requires students to take eight laboratory courses, which generally have to be taken residentially but can be taken at any regionally accredited institution (including one's local community college). One laboratory must be in physics, and the other seven should be in computer technology.

We have also heard word that Excelsior is possibly designing an M.S. in computer information systems or information technology, to be offered by 2003.

Florida State University

Office of Distributed and Distance Learning
University Center, Suite C3500
Tallahassee, FL 32306-2540

Accreditation:	Regional
Year founded:	1851
Ownership:	Nonprofit, state
Phone:	(850) 645 0393 • (877) 357 8283
Email:	students@oddl.fsu.edu
Web site:	www.fsu.edu
Degrees offered:	Bachelor of Science (B.S.) in computer science (coursework-based)
	Bachelor of Science (B.S.) in information studies (coursework-based)
	Bachelor of Science (B.S.) in software engineering (coursework-based)
	Master of Science (M.S.) in information and library studies (coursework-based/thesis required)

Florida State University offers bachelor's completion programs and an M.S. in information and library studies entirely through online study, with no required on-campus residency. Students applying for the bachelor's completion programs must hold an associate's degree or the equivalent.

The B.S. completion programs in computer science and software engineering overlap considerably, drawing from the same 48-semester-hour pool of major coursework but differing in their core distribution requirements. The computer science major focuses largely on computer science theory, computational mathematics, artificial intelligence, and database theory, but also addresses issues in networking and software engineering. The software engineering major focuses on object-oriented programming, operating systems, and concurrent programming, but may also address databases, artificial intelligence, and computer science theory.

The B.S. in information studies is an interdisciplinary program addressing library and information science, communication and group dynamics, and computer science and digital media technologies. Although the focus of the program is largely on information science and organizational communication, courses are offered in multimedia, computer graphics, interface design, and telecommunications. Students may take a one- or two-semester industry internship as part of the program.

The 42-semester-hour M.S. in information and library studies is primarily focused on library science, but can also address topics such as network multimedia, Web site development, information retrieval, computer applications in library science, telecommunications, and network administration. A thesis is required. Although the program can be completed mostly by distance learning, some courses may require residencies.

Franklin University

201 South Grant Avenue
Columbus, OH 43215

Accreditation:	Regional
Year founded:	1902
Ownership:	Independent
Phone:	(888) 341 6237
Email:	alliance@franklin.edu
Web site:	www.alliance.franklin.edu
Degrees offered:	Bachelor of Science (B.S.) in computer science (coursework-based)
	Bachelor of Science (B.S.) in management information systems (coursework-based)
	Bachelor of Science (B.S.) in technical management (coursework-based)

Franklin University offers a variety of online bachelor's programs in cooperation with an alliance of Ohio community colleges.

The B.S. in computer science is a 130-semester-hour program with a whopping 80-hour major in computer science comprised of a 44-hour core and 36-hour specialization. The core focuses on basic principles of computer science, computer architecture, database management, and software engineering; specializations are available in computer engineering (addressing such topics as real time programming, digital systems, and data communications), management information systems (focusing primarily on business and accounting-related courses), and software engineering (focusing on basic principles of computer programming, and allowing students to choose their own programming languages as part of a 16-hour elective credit distribution area).

The B.S. in management information systems is a 127-hour program with a 77-hour major in management information systems. The major is comprised of three parts: a 20-hour business core (which addresses every major area of business, including management information systems, in a survey fashion), a 41-hour focus on management information systems (focusing on databases, computer science, Web site development, human-computer interaction, project management, e-commerce, and telecommunications), and a 16-hour concentration in e-commerce (with special implementation-oriented or marketing-oriented tracks), financial systems, process management and auditing, or an individualized, faculty-approved field of specialization.

The B.S. in technical management is a 130-hour program with 24 hours of required elective courses in technology-related subjects and a 36-hour major. The major focuses on organizational and project management as applied to technology-related industry.

An M.S. in computer science is under development and may be offered in an online format.

Georgia Institute of Technology

Center for Distance Learning
Atlanta, GA 30332

Accreditation:	Regional
Year founded:	1885
Ownership:	Nonprofit, state
Phone:	(404) 894 8572
Fax:	(404) 894 8924
Email:	cdl@conted.gatech.edu
Web site:	www.conted.gatech.edu/distance
Degrees offered:	Master of Science (M.S.) in electrical and computer engineering (coursework-based/project optional)

Georgia Tech has offered nontraditional master's programs for years, and it is now possible to complete an entire degree program through online (or videocassette-based) courses.

The M.S. in electrical and computer engineering involves 30 semester hours of coursework: one 9-hour primary specialization in computer engineering, power/systems and controls, or telecommunications and digital signal processing; one 6-hour secondary specialization (in one of the two remaining fields); one 3-hour elective course in electrical and computer engineering; 6 hours of elective courses in a field not related to electrical and computer engineering; and 6 hours of free electives.

Golden Gate University

536 Mission Street
San Francisco, CA 94105

Accreditation:	Regional
Year founded:	1901
Ownership:	Nonprofit, independent
Phone:	(415) 369 5250 • (888) 874 2923
Fax:	(415) 227 4502
Email:	cybercampus@ggu.edu
Web site:	cybercampus.ggu.edu
Degrees offered:	Master of Science (M.S.) in telecommunications management (coursework-based)

Golden Gate University offers many online master's degree programs through its CyberCampus initiative.

The M.S. in telecommunications management is a 42-semester-hour program designed for IT and telecom professionals. The program is organized around 9 hours of core coursework (telecommunications management, strategic telecommunications, and future of telecommunications), a 15-hour cross-disciplinary component or an optional concentration (in communications technology, networking technology, or telecommunications business management and policy), and 9 hours of electives. Through careful choice of concentration and elective classes, it is quite possible to do a program focused almost entirely on Internet-related telecommunications issues.

Harvard University

Division of Continuing Education
51 Brattle Street
Cambridge, MA 02138

Accreditation: Regional
Year founded: 1636
Ownership: Nonprofit, independent
Phone: (617) 495 4024
Fax: (617) 495 0500
Email: ext@hudce.harvard.edu
Web site: extension.dce.harvard.edu
Degrees offered: Master of Liberal Arts (A.L.M.) in information technology
(coursework-based/project required)

Harvard University now offers hundreds of courses online through its Extension
School, including many of the courses required for the Master of Liberal Arts
program. Although a few required courses are not available online, the number
of residential-only courses in this program keeps dwindling each year.

The program itself consists of five required courses (algorithms and data structures,
communication protocols and Internet architectures, design patterns and Java, Java
for distributed computing, theory of computation and its applications, and Unix
systems programming), four elective courses (in fields such as distributed object
computing with Java and CORBA, artificial intelligence, cryptography, Perl Web
programming, computer graphics, compiler design, digital libraries and the
Internet, and information systems management), and a capstone project.

Iowa State University

Department of Electrical and Computer Engineering
2215 Coover Hall
Iowa State University
Ames, IA 50011

Accreditation:	Regional
Year founded:	1858
Ownership:	Nonprofit, state
Phone:	(515) 294 2663
Fax:	(515) 294 3637
Email:	ece@ee.iastate.edu
Web site:	www.eng.iastate.edu/ede
Degrees offered:	Master of Science (M.S.) in computer engineering (coursework-based/thesis or project required)

Iowa State University, home of the world's first digital computer, offers several engineering programs entirely through online and videocassette-based study.

The 30-semester-hour M.S. in computer engineering follows an individualized, faculty-approved program of study. The program may culminate in a thesis or, if the student prefers, a capstone project.

ISIM University

501 South Cherry Street
Room 350 – Admissions Office
Denver, CO 80246

Accreditation:	National (DETC)
Year founded:	1987
Ownership:	Proprietary
Phone:	(303) 333 4224 • (800) 441 4746
Fax:	(303) 336 1144
Email:	admissions@isim.edu
Web site:	www.isim.edu
Degrees offered:	Master of Science (M.S.) in information management (coursework-based/project required) Master of Science (M.S.) in information technology (coursework-based/thesis or project required)

ISIM University offers unique master's programs in business and computer fields entirely through online study.

The 36-semester-hour M.S. in information management is comprised of three parts: a 24-hour core (addressing telecommunications, emerging technologies, business ethics, project management, organizational behavior, and management-related issues), 9 hours of "free" credits (either electives or a concentration in project management or technologies), and an individualized capstone project.

The 36-hour M.S. in information technology is based on the same model: a 24-hour core (addressing largely the same issues, but with greater emphasis on networking and less emphasis on management), 9 hours of "free" credits (either electives or a concentration in project management), and an individualized capstone project.

ISIM is accredited by the Distance Education and Training Council (DETC), a recognized national accrediting body; all other U.S.-based schools profiled in this book are accredited by one of the six U.S. regional accrediting agencies. For more information on the DETC, see chapter 5.

Judson College

302 Bibb Street
Marion, AL 36756

Accreditation:	Regional
Year founded:	1838
Ownership:	Nonprofit, church
Phone:	(334) 683 5169 • (800) 447 9472
Fax:	(334) 683 5147
Email:	adultstudies@future.judson.edu
Web site:	www.judson.edu
Degrees offered:	Bachelor of Arts or Science (B.A., B.S.) in business administration and management information systems (coursework-based/template-based)
	Bachelor of Arts or Science (B.A., B.S.) with an interdisciplinary major (coursework-based/template-based)

Judson College offers a variety of wholly nonresident bachelor's degrees to women over the age of 21 through an individualized program of study based on a learning contract. Credit is available for prior learning through portfolio assessment, standard equivalency examinations, and proficiency tests prepared by Judson faculty.

Because of the individualized nature of the programs, specific course distribution requirements vary depending on the learning contract agreed upon by the student and Judson faculty.

Kansas State University

13 College Court
Manhattan, KS 66506

Accreditation: Regional
Year founded: 1863
Ownership: Nonprofit, state
Phone: (785) 532 5686 • (800) 622 2578
Fax: (785) 532 5637
Email: info@dce.ksu.edu
Web site: www.dce.ksu.edu
Degrees offered: Master of Software Engineering (M.Sw.E.)
(coursework-based/project required)

Kansas State University offers a number of master's degrees through its Division
of Continuing Education. Courses are primarily offered online, supplemented as
appropriate with correspondence, CD-ROMs, audiocassettes, and videotapes.

The Master of Software Engineering is a 33-semester-hour program comprised of
a 9-hour core in software engineering and software management, 6 hours of field
electives (chosen from courses in fields such as software measurement, database
design, protocol engineering, reactive systems, and data engineering), 6 hours in an
application area (an individualized, faculty-approved track or any of the following:
chemical engineering, computer engineering, database engineering, electrical engineering, graphics, industrial engineering, knowledge-based systems, mechanical
engineering, nuclear engineering, operating systems and real time systems, or parallel and distributed systems), a 6-hour project, and 6 hours of technical electives in
another field (such as computer science or an interdisciplinary application area).

Keller Graduate School of Management

One Tower Lane
Oakbrook Terrace, IL 60181

Accreditation:	Regional
Year founded:	1973
Ownership:	Proprietary
Phone:	(630) 574 1960 • (888) 535 5378
Fax:	(630) 574 1969
Email:	sbranick@keller.edu
Web site:	www.keller.edu
Degrees offered:	Master of Information Systems Management (coursework-based/project required)
	Master of Telecommunications Management (coursework-based)

Keller now offers many of its master's degree programs in an online format, as well as certificate programs in a number of fields (including e-commerce management, information systems management, and telecommunications management).

The Master of Information Systems Management requires 60 quarter hours (40 semester hours) of work, distributed as follows: 42 quarter hours of flexible core courses available in fields such as C++ programming, Java programming, Internet-oriented programming, Visual Basic, COBOL, databases, networking, project management, and a number of management-related fields; a 12-hour emphasis in distributed systems, electronic commerce, or large systems; and a 6-hour capstone project.

The Master of Telecommunications Management also requires 60 quarter hours of work; all of it falls under the basic heading of core coursework, although some flexibility is allowed. Coursework emphasizes management issues, strategic technology management, networking, telecommunications law, databases, and project management.

Lakeland College

P.O. Box 359
Sheboygan, WI 53082

Accreditation: Regional
Year founded: 1862
Ownership: Nonprofit, independent
Phone: (920) 565 2111
Fax: (920) 565 1206
Email: online@lakeland.edu
Web site: www.lakeland.edu
Degrees offered: Bachelor of Arts (B.A.) in computer science
(coursework-based)

Lakeland College's B.A. in computer science is offered entirely through online coursework. Up to 92 hours of credit from another regionally accredited institution may count toward the 128-semester-hour degree.

The 30-hour major in computer science requires courses in business information systems, databases, systems analysis, COBOL, and C++ programming. Elective courses are available in advanced COBOL and C++ programming, Visual Basic, and data structures.

Lesley University

29 Everett Street
Cambridge, MA 02138-2790

Accreditation:	Regional
Year founded:	1909
Ownership:	Nonprofit, independent
Phone:	(617) 349 8320 • (800) 999 1959
Fax:	(617) 349 8313
Email:	info@mail.lesley.edu
Web site:	www.lesley.edu
Degrees offered:	Master of Arts (M.A.) in independent study (any field) (template-based)

Lesley University offers an individualized M.A. through its Independent Study Degree Program (ISDP). Students work with faculty advisors (some of them chosen by the student from industry or academia) to create an individualized program of study in virtually any field. This is the only individualized M.A. program described in this book that can be completed entirely online with no on-campus residency.

An M.Ed. and M.S. in educational technology are also available through this model.

Marlboro College

Vernon Street, Suite 5
Brattleboro, VT 05301

Accreditation: Regional
Year founded: 1946
Ownership: Nonprofit, independent
Phone: (802) 258 9200 • (888) 258 5665
Fax: (802) 258 9201
Email: gradcenter@marlboro.edu
Web site: www.gradcenter.marlboro.edu
Degrees offered: Master of Science (M.S.) in Internet engineering
(coursework-based/project required)
Master of Science (M.S.) in Internet strategy management
(coursework-based/project required)

The Graduate Center of Marlboro College offers several master's programs through a mix of online study and short residencies (two weekends each month). In addition to the programs described above, an M.A. in teaching (with emphasis on Internet instruction) is available through this model.

The M.S. in Internet engineering is a 30-semester-hour program designed for working professionals who already have a solid programming background. The curriculum involves courses in relevant database systems (6 hours), Internet programming (9 hours), Internet technologies (6 hours), and Web site engineering (3 hours); the program concludes with a significant capstone project.

The 30-hour M.S. in Internet strategy management involves courses in Internet law and ethics (3 hours), Internet marketing (3 hours), network systems (3 hours), technology management (6 hours), Web application development (3 hours), and Web site design (6 hours). The program concludes with a capstone project.

Mercy College

555 Broadway
Dobbs Ferry, NY 10522

Accreditation:	Regional
Year founded:	1950
Ownership:	Nonprofit, independent
Phone:	(914) 693 7600 • (800) 637 2969
Fax:	(914) 674 7382
Email:	admissions@merlin.mercynet.edu
Web site:	merlin.mercynet.edu
Degrees offered:	Bachelor of Science (B.S.) in computer science (coursework-based)

Mercy College offers several online degree programs through the Mercy Long-distance Instructional Network (MerLIN).

The online B.S. in computer science is designed primarily for students who already possess an associate's degree or the equivalent, but students who don't may earn their associate's online through MerLIN. Coursework represents a fairly balanced and traditional computer science curriculum, with roughly equal weight on theory and software issues.

We have heard that Mercy's M.S. in Internet business systems may be available online, either now or within the near future; contact the school for details.

Mississippi State University

Office of Graduate Studies
116 Allen Hall
P.O. Box G
Mississippi State, MS 39762

Accreditation:	Regional
Year founded:	1878
Ownership:	Nonprofit, state
Phone:	(662) 325 7400
Email:	grad@grad.msstate.edu
Web site:	www.msstate.edu
Degrees offered:	Master of Science (M.S.) in computer engineering (coursework-based/thesis optional)
	Master of Science (M.S.) in computer science (coursework-based/thesis or project required)

Mississippi State University offers master's programs in about a dozen fields entirely by distance learning (generally online study, although videocourses are available for students who lack the necessary computer requirements).

The 30- to 33-semester-hour M.S. in computer engineering involves 9 hours of electrical and computer engineering credit, 9 hours of computer science credit, and 6 (for the thesis track) or 18 (for the non-thesis track) hours of elective courses.

The 32-hour M.S. in computer science is centered on an individualized, faculty-approved area of study (common areas of study: advanced scientific computing, artificial intelligence, computer architecture, database systems, graphics and visualization, high performance computing, programming languages and systems, and software engineering). Students must complete 26 hours of coursework and a 6-hour thesis or project.

Monash University

Distance Education Centre
Gippsland Campus
Northways Road
Churchill, Victoria 3842
Australia

Accreditation:	International (GAAP)
Year founded:	1961
Ownership:	State
Phone:	+61 (3) 9902 6200
Fax:	+61 (3) 9902 6300
Email:	de@monash.edu.au
Web site:	www.monash.edu.au/de
Degrees offered:	Bachelor of Business and Electronic Commerce (coursework-based)
	Bachelor of Computing (coursework-based/project required)
	Bachelor of Multimedia Computing (coursework-based/project required)
	Master of Business Systems (coursework-based/project optional)
	Master of Information Management and Systems (coursework-based)
	Master of Information Technology (coursework-based/thesis or project required)
	Master of Multimedia Computing (coursework-based/project optional)
	Master of Network Computing (coursework-based/project optional)

Monash University offers the above programs entirely through distance-learning methods (such as audio- and videotape, written lessons, online study, and correspondence) to students worldwide.

The Bachelor of Business and Electronic Commerce consists of 24 modules: a core of 18 modules (8 in e-commerce, 10 in business) and 6 modules comprising a specialization in one of the following fields: accounting, business law, economics, management, marketing, or tourism management.

The Bachelor of Computing consists of 23 modules: a core of 15 modules (including an industry project and courses in databases, object-oriented programming, and software engineering) and 8 elective modules (in fields such as computer graphics, e-commerce infrastructure, human-computer interaction, multimedia, Unix, and Web databases).

The Bachelor of Multimedia Computing is also divided between a 15-module core (including a multimedia project and courses in various aspects of multimedia technology) and eight electives. The 12-module master's in this field further explores GUI design, multimedia Java programming, computer graphics, computer vision and image processing, e-commerce, and multimedia protocols.

The Master of Business Systems covers such fields as business statistics, e-commerce, evolutionary and neural computing, and multimedia computing.

The Master of Information Management and Systems includes such specializations as decision support systems, electronic recordkeeping and archiving, information management, information systems development, information technology management, library and information services, and multimedia.

The Master of Information Technology consists of 8 modules taken from a list of approved subjects (including e-commerce, GUI development, Java, multimedia programming, multimedia protocols, and online trading systems) and at least 4 elective modules (in fields such as computer vision and image processing, evolutionary and neural computing, inventory management systems, and software system design). A thesis (approximately four semesters, and of at least 15,000 words) or project (one to two semesters) is required.

For the Master of Network Computing, also 12 modules, students may undertake a project in lieu of 2 modules.

Murdoch University

External Studies Unit
90 South Street
Murdoch, Western Australia 6150
Australia

Accreditation:	International (GAAP)
Year founded:	1973
Ownership:	Nonprofit, state
Phone:	+61 (8) 9360 2498
Email:	p_martin@cleo.murdoch.edu.au
Web site:	www.murdoch.edu.au
Degrees offered:	Bachelor of Science (B.S.) in applied computational physics (coursework-based)
	Bachelor of Science (B.S.) in computer science (coursework-based)

Murdoch University offers a variety of master's programs by distance learning to students worldwide. Instruction takes place through online study or correspondence augmented by other appropriate media (videocassettes, audiocassettes, and so forth).

The B.S. in applied computational physics generally takes three to five years to complete. Students may choose a general track or specialize in computer science, energy studies, environmental applications, mathematical physics, mineral processing, or physics. Qualified students may take on an additional year of study to convert the B.S. into an Honours program.

The B.S. in computer science involves 28 modules and generally takes three to five years to complete. Students may undertake a 4-module specialization in Internet computing or software development. Qualified students may also take on an additional year of study to convert the B.S. into an Honours program.

A graduate diploma in computer studies is also available; students must pass a total of eight units (six required, two elective).

National Technological University

700 Centre Avenue
Fort Collins, CO 80526

Accreditation: Regional
Year founded: 1984
Ownership: Nonprofit, independent
Phone: (970) 495 6400 • (800) 582 9976
Fax: (970) 484 0668
Email: admissions@mail.ntu.edu
Web site: www.ntu.edu
Degrees offered: Master of Science (M.S.) in computer engineering
(coursework-based)
Master of Science (M.S.) in computer science
(coursework-based)
Master of Science (M.S.) in information systems
(coursework-based)
Master of Science (M.S.) in software engineering
(coursework-based)

In cooperation with 45 regionally accredited institutions nationwide, National Technological University offers the above programs (and many others) entirely through online study or, if the student prefers, satellite digital compressed video.

The 30-semester-hour M.S. in computer engineering involves 8 hours of core coursework within the broad areas of algorithms, data structures, computer architecture, and software engineering; a 10.5-hour concentration in any two of the following: algorithms and data structures, computer architecture, computational methods and theory, computer software, digital systems, intelligent systems, software engineering, or software techniques; 5 hours of breadth courses in a field other than computer engineering; and 6.5 hours of electives. No thesis or project is required.

The 30-hour M.S. in computer science involves 15 hours of core coursework within the broad areas of algorithms, data structures, computational methods and theory, computer architecture, intelligent systems, and software engineering; a 9-hour concentration in algorithms and data structures, computational methods and theory, computer architecture, computer software, intelligent systems, software engineering, or software techniques; and 6 hours of electives. No thesis or project is required.

The 33-hour M.S. in software engineering involves 18 hours of core coursework in five or more of the following: analysis and design techniques, life cycle models and software metrics, productivity measures and quality assurance, programming environments and implementation issues, software engineering methodology, software management/psychology and control methods, specification languages and other language issues, and testing and reliability; 6 hours of depth coursework in computer software, intelligent systems, software engineering, or software techniques; a 3-hour extradisciplinary course in algorithms and data structures, computer architecture, computational methods and theory, digital systems, management and behavioral science, or mathematics; and 6 hours of electives. No thesis or project is required.

National University

11255 North Torrey Pines Road
La Jolla, CA 92037-1011

Accreditation:	Regional
Year founded:	1971
Ownership:	Nonprofit, independent
Phone:	(619) 563 7100
Fax:	(619) 642 8714
Email:	getinfo@nu.edu
Web site:	www.nu.edu
Degrees offered:	Master of Science (M.S.) in electronic commerce (coursework-based/research project required)

National University offers both standard and highly innovative programs entirely through online study.

The online M.S. in electronic commerce involves 10 courses (addressing issues such as graphic design, Web-based applications, telecommunications, database management, global network marketing, and electronic payment systems) and a two-semester final research project. The program is generally expected to take two to three years to complete.

Naval Postgraduate School

1 University Circle
Monterey, CA 93943

Accreditation:	Regional
Year founded:	1909
Ownership:	Nonprofit, state
Phone:	(831) 656 2441
Fax:	(831) 656 2921
Email:	grad-ed@nps.navy.mil
Web site:	www.nps.navy.mil
Degrees offered:	Master of Science (M.S.) in software engineering (coursework-based)

The Naval Postgraduate School offers a variety of engineering-related master's programs to Department of Defense employees worldwide through video tele-conferencing technology.

The M.S. in software engineering involves 28 courses (16 regular courses, 12 lecture courses) and a thesis. Coursework addresses such topics as economic evaluation of information systems, software testing, computer communications networking, software reuse, software evolution, software research and development in the Department of Defense, software prototyping, and embedded real-time systems. The program is designed to be completed in about two years.

A master's in electrical engineering is also available and can be tailored (to a certain extent) to computer engineering issues.

New Jersey Institute of Technology

Office of Distance Learning
University Heights, NJ 07102

Accreditation: Regional
Year founded: 1881
Ownership: Nonprofit, state
Phone: (973) 596 3177 • (800) 624 9850
Fax: (973) 596 3203
Email: dl@njit.edu
Web site: www.njit.edu
Degrees offered: Bachelor of Science (B.S.) in computer science
(coursework-based/project required)
Bachelor of Science (B.S.) in information systems
(coursework-based)

NJIT offers entire degree programs through distance learning using videotaped courses, online conferencing, fax, and phone. Distance students study on the same schedule as on-campus students, and examinations can be administered in remote locations by an approved proctor. Students must have Internet access.

The ABET-accredited B.S. in computer science involves a rigorous curriculum in the natural sciences and mathematics. Core coursework addresses Assembly language programming, computer architecture, logic and automata, software engineering, operating systems, databases, and other topics. Elective courses are available in artificial intelligence, management information systems, data communications, object-oriented programming, human-computer interaction, computer graphics, Unix, and other fields.

The B.S. major in information systems is actually quite similar to the computer science major, but involves fewer theory- and programming-oriented courses and more management-oriented courses. Coursework addresses computer applications to commercial problems, organizational behavior, databases, management information systems, financial management, system design, Assembly language programming, and other topics. Elective courses are available in most of the fields listed for computer science (above).

Norwich University

Vermont College
College Street
Montpelier, VT 05602

Accreditation:	Regional
Year founded:	1834
Ownership:	Nonprofit, independent
Phone:	(802) 828 8500 • (800) 336 6794
Fax:	(802) 828 8855
Email:	vcadmis@norwich.edu
Web site:	www.norwich.edu/vermontcollege
Degrees offered:	Bachelor of Arts (B.A.) in any field (template-based)
	Master of Arts (M.A.) in any field (template-based/thesis required)

Vermont College of Norwich University offers some of the longest-running external degree programs in North America for adult students.

The individualized B.A. is based on a learning contract between the student and a faculty mentor. Each semester involves a significant amount of preliminary study and concludes with a culminating study project. Credit for prior learning (transfer credit, credit by examinations, and life-experience evaluation) is available. Students spend one week per six months on campus, or the equivalent in weekend residencies.

The individualized M.A. is similar in approach; students choose a committee of two supervisors (one from Vermont College, and an external academic or industry supervisor who is an expert in the proposed field of study). This program can be completed almost entirely off-campus; by using online communication options, a student can reduce the residency requirement to a single initial five-day colloquium. A thesis is required.

Nova Southeastern University

3301 College Avenue
Fort Lauderdale, FL 33314

Accreditation: Regional
Year founded: 1964
Ownership: Nonprofit, independent
Phone: (954) 262 2000 • (800) 986 2247
Email: scisinfo@nova.edu
Web site: www.scis.nova.edu
Degrees offered: Master of Science (M.S.) in computer information systems
(coursework-based/thesis or project optional)
Master of Science (M.S.) in computer science
(coursework-based/thesis or project optional)
Master of Science (M.S.) in computing technology in education
(coursework-based/thesis or project optional)
Master of Science (M.S.) in management information systems
(coursework-based/thesis or project optional)
Doctor of Philosophy (Ph.D.) in computer information systems
(coursework-based/four projects/dissertation)
Doctor of Philosophy (Ph.D.) in computer sciences
(coursework-based/four projects/dissertation)
Doctor of Philosophy (Ph.D.) or Doctor of Education (Ed.D.)
in computing technology in education
(coursework-based/four projects/dissertation)
Doctor of Philosophy (Ph.D.) in information systems
(coursework-based/four projects/dissertation)

Nova Southeastern University offers a variety of online and low-residency degree programs to students nationwide. All of the master's programs listed above may be completed entirely through online study; the doctoral programs require students to attend occasional residencies with regional cluster groups.

The master's programs in computer information systems, computer science, and management information systems all consist of 36 semester hours of study: 30 hours in core courses and 6 hours of electives. The computer information systems and computer science degrees cover many of the same topics (operating systems, data communications, object-oriented programming, software engineering, etc.), although the computer science program does place more emphasis on programming and theory (with courses in algorithms and artificial intelligence). The M.S. in management information systems covers such areas as project management, data warehousing, e-commerce, systems analysis, and decision support systems.

The M.S. in computer technology in education consists of twelve courses addressing such fields as instructional delivery systems, networks, integrated applications, multimedia, learning theory, and human-computer interaction. A thesis or project may substitute two courses.

The Ph.D. programs all follow a model of eight core courses, four project courses, and a dissertation.

Oklahoma City University

PLUS Program
2501 North Blackwelder
Oklahoma City, OK 73106-1493

Accreditation:	Regional
Year founded:	1901
Ownership:	Nonprofit, state
Phone:	(405) 521 5265
Email:	plus@okcu.edu
Web site:	www.okcu.edu/plus
Degrees offered:	Bachelor of Arts (B.A.) or Bachelor of Science (B.S.) in any field (template-based)

A B.A. or B.S. degree in any field can be earned by utilizing a combination of alternative methods: independent study, seminars, assessment of prior learning, and traditional courses. Each student must visit the campus to attend an orientation workshop, and additional campus visits may be necessary (depending on the field of study and other relevant factors).

The university has asked us to point out that while the program may be suitable for some distance students, it may not meet the needs of others. An evaluation of each student's educational situation is necessary.

Park University

8700 River Park Drive
Parkville, MO 64152

Accreditation: Regional
Year founded: 1875
Ownership: Nonprofit, church
Phone: (816) 741 2000 • (800) 745 7275
Fax: (816) 746 6423
Email: admissions@mail.park.edu
Web site: www.park.edu
Degrees offered: Bachelor of Science (B.S.) in computer information systems and management
(coursework-based)

Park University offers a B.S. completion program in computer information systems
almost entirely through online distance learning. Students must hold an associate's
degree or the equivalent (about 60 semester hours of credit from a regionally
accredited school). Two courses must be taken in a classroom setting, either on
campus at Park College or on one of Park's many extension sites (located on or near
military bases around the country). Courses address such topics as artificial intelligence,
management information systems, computer systems analysis and design,
and networks and data communications.

Regent University

1000 Regent University Drive
Virginia Beach, VA 23464-9800

Accreditation: Regional
Year founded: 1977
Ownership: Nonprofit
Phone: (757) 226 4127 • (800) 373 5504
Fax: (757) 424 7051
Email: admissions@regent.edu
Web site: www.regent.edu
Degrees offered: Master of Arts (M.A.) in communication, with emphasis in computer-mediated communication (coursework-based/thesis or project or examination required)

Regent University offers a variety of programs through nonresident and low-residency formats. Founded as CBN University (named after university founder Pat Robertson's Christian Broadcasting Network), Regent University integrates traditional Judeo-Christian ethical principles in the teaching of its courses.

The M.A. in communication, with emphasis in computer-mediated communication, can be completed entirely online with no on-campus residency whatsoever. The program consists of 39 semester hours of coursework (13 courses) and a culminating project (thesis, creative portfolio, or comprehensive examination). Students move through the program using a cohort model (fairly unusual for a fully online program). The 33 hours of required courses focus on a variety of interdisciplinary fields (ethics of communication, aesthetics and design of computer-mediated communication projects, communication and technology, and so forth); the student directs the remaining 6 hours toward a specialization in business (e-commerce and electronic marketing), communication arts (computer-mediated communication techniques and advanced Web site development), divinity (theology of computer-mediated communication and the church online), education (computer-mediated education and online pedagogy), or law (online intellectual property or telecommunications/Internet law).

The online M.A. in management and MBA programs are also available with an e-business specialization.

Regis University

School for Professional Studies
3333 Regis Boulevard
Denver, CO 80221

Accreditation:	Regional
Year founded:	1877
Ownership:	Nonprofit, church
Phone:	(303) 458 4080 • (800) 677 9270
Fax:	(303) 964 5538
Email:	masters@regis.edu
Web site:	www.regis.edu
Degrees offered:	Master of Science (M.S.) in computer information systems (coursework-based/project required)

This respected Jesuit school offers many degrees online through its School for Professional Studies, including an M.S. in computer information systems.

This 36-semester-hour program, offered in consultation with Sun Microsystems, is probably the single most cutting-edge and flexible online master's available in the field. The program consists of a 9-hour core in applied systems analysis, computer systems architecture, and presentation of technical materials; a 12-hour concentration in a faculty-approved individualized field or one of the following: database technologies, e-commerce engineering, networking technologies, object-oriented technologies, or technology management; 12 hours of elective credit; and a 3-hour capstone project. This program can be completed in about two years of part-time study.

Online graduate certificate programs are also available in database technologies, networking, and object-oriented technologies.

Rensselaer Polytechnic Institute

Professional and Distance Education
CII Suite 4011
110 8th Street
Troy, NY 12180-3590

Accreditation:	Regional
Year founded:	1824
Ownership:	Nonprofit, independent
Phone:	(518) 276 7787
Fax:	(518) 276 8026
Email:	rsvp@rpi.edu
Web site:	www.rsvp.rpi.edu
Degrees offered:	Master of Engineering (M.Eng.) in computer and systems engineering (coursework-based/project required)
	Master of Science (M.S.) in computer science (coursework-based)
	Master of Science (M.S.) in information technology (coursework-based)

Rensselaer Polytechnic Institute offers a number of degree programs and certificates by distance learning through the RSVP program. Students may complete degree requirements online or through videocourses, or through two-way streaming video at corporate sites.

The Master of Engineering (M.Eng.) in computer and systems engineering involves 30 semester hours of study: a 9-hour concentration in computer networking or software engineering, a 6-hour two-course sequence in a related professional field, 9–12 hours of electives, and a 3–6 hour final project.

The 30-hour M.S. in computer science involves 7 hours of required core courses (compatibility and complexity, and operating systems), 3–4 hours of software development coursework, 3–4 hours of applications coursework, a 3-hour research methods course, a 1-hour seminar course, and 7–10 hours of electives.

The 30-hour M.S. in information technology involves 16–18 hours of core courses covering database systems, human-computer interaction, management of technology, software design, and telecommunications, and a 12–16 hour specialization in database systems design, human-computer interaction, information systems engineering, networking, or software engineering and design.

RPI also offers an M.S. and M.Eng. in electrical engineering with a concentration in microelectronics.

Rochester Institute of Technology

91 Lomb Memorial Drive
Rochester, NY 14623-5603

Accreditation: Regional
Year founded: 1829
Ownership: Nonprofit, independent
Phone: (716) 475 5089 • (800) 225 5748
Fax: (716) 475 5077
Email: online@rit.edu
Web site: distancelearning.rit.edu
Degrees offered: Bachelor of Science (B.S.) in applied arts and sciences
(coursework-based)
Bachelor of Science (B.S.) in telecommunications engineering technology
(coursework-based)
Master of Science (M.S.) in cross-disciplinary professional studies
(coursework-based/thesis or project required)
Master of Science (M.S.) in imaging science
(coursework-based/project required)
Master of Science (M.S.) in information technology
(coursework-based/thesis or project required)
Master of Science (M.S.) in microelectronics manufacturing engineering
(coursework-based/internship required)
Master of Science (M.S.) in software development and management
(coursework-based/project required)

Rochester Institute of Technology offers the above programs almost entirely
through online study, although short laboratory seminars are sometimes required.

The B.S. in applied arts and sciences is a highly flexible program designed primarily
for adult learners. Students choose an emphasis in applied computing, digital imaging and publishing, e-business, or telecommunications. Credit is available for prior
learning (transfer credit, credit by examination, military training, professional training, and life-experience evaluation), although at least 45 quarter hours (30 semester
hours) must be earned through RIT.

The B.S. completion program in telecommunications engineering technology
requires that students hold an associate's degree or the equivalent (90 quarter
hours/60 semester hours of credit). Coursework focuses on networking, microelectronics, databases, and telecom policy.

Master's programs generally require 48 quarter hours of study and a capstone project or thesis. The M.S. in microelectronics manufacturing engineering requires an
internship in the semiconductor industry.

St. Mary-of-the-Woods College

Women's External Degree (WED) Program
Saint Mary-of-the-Woods, IN 47876

Accreditation:	Regional
Year founded:	1840
Ownership:	Nonprofit, church
Phone:	(812) 535 5106 • (800) 926 7692
Email:	adm-smwc@smwc.edu
Web site:	www.smwc.edu
Degrees offered:	Bachelor of Science (B.S.) in accounting information systems (coursework-based/template-based)
	Bachelor of Science (B.S.) in computer information systems (coursework-based/template-based/project optional)
	Bachelor of Science (B.S.) in digital media communication (coursework-based/template-based)
	Bachelor of Science (B.S.) in any field (coursework-based/template-based/project optional)

St. Mary-of-the-Woods College offers a variety of programs through off-campus independent study, punctuated with brief on-campus residencies (an average of one day per semester). Credit for prior learning is awarded through portfolio examination, and some transfer credit is accepted. Only women are eligible for the programs described here.

The B.S. in accounting information systems is a 150-semester-hour program with a triple-field concentration in accounting (36 hours), business (27 hours), and computer information systems (15 hours). The accounting concentration is designed to prepare students for the CPA examination. The computer information systems concentration focuses on databases, Visual Basic programming, and computer systems engineering.

For the 125-semester-hour B.S. in computer information systems, the major is comprised of two parts: an 18-hour core (which involves 9 hours of programming focusing largely on C/C++, 6 hours of databases, and one survey course) and a specialization in computer systems technology (23 hours) or Internet technology (24 hours).

The B.S. in digital media communication is a 125-semester-hour program with a 36-hour double-field concentration in communication (12 hours) and digital media communication and journalism (24 hours).

The individualized B.S. focuses on a student-defined, faculty-approved curriculum; students may design a program in virtually any field.

Skidmore College

University Without Walls
815 North Broadway
Saratoga Springs, NY 12866

Accreditation: Regional
Year founded: 1911
Ownership: Nonprofit, independent
Phone: (518) 580 5450
Fax: (518) 580 5449
Email: uww@skidmore.edu
Web site: www.skidmore.edu
Degrees offered: Bachelor of Arts (B.A.) or Bachelor of Science (B.S.) in any field (template-based)

Skidmore is one of the pioneers of nontraditional education, having offered a University Without Walls program since 1970. Only three days are required on campus: one for an admissions interview, a second for advising and planning, and a third to present a degree plan to a faculty committee. Skidmore makes it clear that they hold their graduates to "standards of knowledge, competence, and intellectual attainment which are no less comprehensive and rigorous than those established by traditional . . . programs." In addition to fulfilling all other requirements in the degree program, each student completes a final project demonstrating competence in his or her field.

All majors are individualized, faculty-approved study plans, but may be patterned after Skidmore's on-campus computer-related offerings (a major in computer science is available) or a field of the student's choice (the Web page makes reference to a previous curriculum in management information systems, but the possibilities are almost endless).

South Bank University

International Office
103 Borough Road
London SE1 0AA
United Kingdom

Accreditation:	International (GAAP)
Year founded:	1970
Ownership:	Nonprofit, state
Phone:	+44 (20) 7815 6137
Fax:	+44 (20) 7815 6199
Web site:	www.southbank-university.ac.uk
Degrees offered:	Master of Philosophy (M.Phil.) in computing (research-based)
	Master of Philosophy (M.Phil.) in geotechnics (research-based)
	Doctor of Philosophy (Ph.D.) in computing (research-based or publication-based)
	Doctor of Philosophy (Ph.D.) in geotechnics (research-based or publication-based)

South Bank University offers research-based programs to students worldwide. Students generally spend six weeks per year on campus, plus the oral defense of the dissertation (which may sometimes be taken in the U.S. under special arrangement). An M.Phil. generally takes two to three years to complete; a Ph.D. four to six years.

It is also possible to be awarded a Ph.D. for published work if one has a "significant connection with the University."

Southern Methodist University

School of Engineering and Applied Science
P.O. Box 750335
Dallas, TX 75205-0335

Accreditation:	Regional
Year founded:	1911
Ownership:	Nonprofit, church
Phone:	(214) 768 3900
Fax:	(214) 768 3778
Email:	tdowning@mail.smu.edu
Web site:	www.seas.smu.edu/disted
Degrees offered:	Master of Science (M.S.) in computer science (coursework-based/thesis optional)
	Master of Science (M.S.) in software engineering (coursework-based)
	Master of Science (M.S.) in telecommunications (coursework-based)

Southern Methodist University has developed a powerful videocassette-based distance-learning program designed for working engineers.

The M.S. in computer science is a 30-semester-hour program with a 15-hour core (addressing algorithms, computer architecture, and operating systems), 9 hours of electives, and the option to pursue a 6-hour thesis or concentration track. Two-course concentrations are available in algorithms, architecture, artificial intelligence, and software.

The M.S. in software engineering is a 30-hour professional program involving a 12-hour core, 9 hours of advanced topic courses (in fields such as software metrics and quaity engineering, user interface design, and software generation and maintenance), and 9 hours of electives. No thesis or project is required.

Following the same basic model as the master's in software engineering, the M.S. in telecommunications covers such fields as digital switching, fiber optic telecommunications, ATM systems, intelligent networks, telecommunications software, and Internet telecommunications. The program can be focused almost exclusively on Internet- and intranet-relevant telecommunications.

Southwest Missouri State University

901 South National Street
Springfield, MO 65804

Accreditation:	Regional
Year founded:	1906
Ownership:	Nonprofit, state
Phone:	(417) 836 4131
Fax:	(417) 836 6907
Email:	mscis@smsu.edu
Web site:	www.mscis.smsu.edu
Degrees offered:	Master of Science (M.S.) in computer information systems (coursework-based)

Southwest Missouri State University's M.S. in computer information systems was ranked 8th in *Computerworld*'s list of "The Top 25 Techno-MBAs"; we note, however, that this is not a purely business-oriented program.

This 36-semester-hour program is designed to be completed in about four semesters (at a rate of three courses per semester); no thesis is required. Thirty hours of the curriculum are set in stone, and the remaining 6 hours are elective. Most courses focus on technology issues such as end-user computing, network administration, comparative system development methodologies, data modeling, and operating systems. Others focus on management-related issues such as organizational transformation, project management, and information systems management.

Southwestern Adventist University

Adult Degree Program
Keene, TX 76059

Accreditation:	Regional
Year founded:	1893
Ownership:	Nonprofit, church
Phone:	(817) 556 4705 • (800) 433 2240
Fax:	(817) 556 4742
Email:	admissions@swau.edu
Web site:	www.swau.edu
Degrees offered:	Bachelor of Arts (B.A.) or Bachelor of Science (B.S.) in any field (predesigned track in computer science available) (template-based)

Southwestern Adventist University's Adult Degree Program (ADP) offers a highly nontraditional individualized bachelor's completion program to students age 22 and older who have been out of college for at least one year. Virtually all work can be completed at a distance following a six-day admission seminar (held each March, June, and October). Credit is earned by standardized examinations, credit for prior learning (portfolio), transfer of credit, and independent study (through any appropriate communication media).

Stanford University

Stanford Center for Professional Development
496 Lomita Mall, Durand Building, Room 401
Stanford, CA 94305-4036

Accreditation:	Regional
Year founded:	1885
Ownership:	Nonprofit, independent
Phone:	(650) 725 3000
Fax:	(650) 725 2868
Email:	sitn-registration@stanford.edu
Web site:	stanford-online.stanford.edu
Degrees offered:	Master of Science (M.S.) in electrical engineering, emphasis on telecommunications (coursework-based)

In the fall of 1998, Stanford became the first major U.S. research university to offer a master's degree entirely through Internet study: an M.S. in electrical engineering with an emphasis in telecommunications.

The program consists of 45 semester hours of study (15 courses) in fields such as analog integrated circuit design, Fourier optics, wireless communications, computer systems, fiber optics, digital filtering, VLSI, and logic design.

An M.S. in computer science is also available to corporate and government subscribers through on-site delivery methods supplemented by Stanford's many available online courses in the field.

Strayer University

1025 15th Street Northwest
Washington, DC 20005

Accreditation:	Regional
Year founded:	1892
Ownership:	Proprietary
Phone:	(703) 339 1850 • (800) 422 8055
Fax:	(703) 339 1852
Email:	jct@strayer.edu
Web site:	www.strayer.edu
Degrees offered:	Associate of Science (A.S.) in computer information systems (coursework-based)
	Bachelor of Science (B.S.) in computer information systems (coursework-based)
	Bachelor of Science (B.S.) in computer networking (coursework-based)
	Master of Science (M.S.) in information systems (coursework-based/research project required)

Strayer University offers online associate's, bachelor's, and master's programs in a variety of business- and computer-related fields.

The A.S. and B.S. in computer information systems focus on programming, addressing databases (Oracle and PL/SQL), Visual Basic, networking, and Unix.

The B.S. in computer networking focuses on Unix, network security, and systems analysis, with emphasis on either Microsoft Windows networking or Novell NetWare.

The M.S. in information systems is a 54-quarter-hour program comprised of two parts: an 18-hour component in business and a 36-hour major focusing on simulation and modeling, systems analysis, networking, and databases. A final research project is required.

One-year diploma programs are available in computer information systems, databases (emphasis on Oracle database administration or Oracle database development), networking (emphasis on Microsoft Windows networking or Novell NetWare), and programming (addressing Oracle, PL/SQL, Visual Basic, object-oriented programming, and C).

Syracuse University

Syracuse University Continuing Education
700 University Avenue
Syracuse, NY 13244-2530

Accreditation:	Regional
Year founded:	1870
Ownership:	Nonprofit, independent
Phone:	(315) 443 4590 • (800) 442 0501
Fax:	(315) 443 4174
Email:	suisdp@uc.syr.edu
Web site:	www.yesu.syr.edu
Degrees offered:	Master of Science (M.S.) in information resources management (coursework-based/internship required for some students)
	Master of Science (M.S.) in telecommunications and network management (coursework-based)

Syracuse offers a variety of Independent Study Degree Programs (ISDPs) that combine correspondence and online study with yearly residencies ranging from one to four weeks.

The 42-semester-hour M.S. in information resources management is comprised of three parts: a 16-hour core focusing on management-related issues within the context of information technology and telecommunications; a 20–23 hour three-field distribution requirement in management approaches and strategies, technological infrastructure, and user information needs; and a 3–6 hour internship (waived for students who already have professional experience in the field).

The M.S. in telecommunications and network management follows a similar model; its distribution requirement covers industry and policy, management, and technology.

Texas Tech University

Distance Learning Program
Computer Science Department
P.O. Box 43104
Lubbock, TX 79409-3104

Accreditation:	Regional
Year founded:	1923
Ownership:	Nonprofit, state
Phone:	(806) 742 1189
Fax:	(806) 742 3519
Email:	distlearn@ttu.edu
Web site:	aln.coe.ttu.edu
Degrees offered:	Master of Science (M.S.) in software engineering (coursework-based/project required/thesis optional)

Texas Tech University offers several engineering-related master's degrees entirely through distance learning. Lectures are sent to the student on CD, on videocassette, or by Internet streaming video; students then complete their assignments online.

The M.S. in software engineering involves 24 (for the thesis track) or 36 (for the non-thesis track) semester hours of coursework, including a two-semester studio (project) course and courses on real-time systems, software project management, and software metrics.

Thomas Edison State College

101 West State Street
Trenton, NJ 08608-1176

Accreditation:	Regional
Year founded:	1972
Ownership:	Nonprofit, state
Phone:	(609) 292 6565 • (888) 442 8372
Fax:	(609) 984 8447
Email:	admissions@tesc.edu
Web site:	www.tesc.edu
Degrees offered:	Bachelor of Science (B.S.) in applied science and technology, with emphasis in computer science technology (template-based)
	Bachelor of Arts (B.A.) in computer science (template-based)

As the state-funded external degree program of the state of New Jersey, Thomas Edison State College offers inexpensive, highly flexible degrees in 118 fields with no required on-campus attendance. Sources for credit include Thomas Edison State College's own distance-learning courses, unlimited transfer credit from any other regionally accredited institution, unlimited credit for life experience through portfolio evaluations, unlimited credit by examination, and credit awarded for prior ACE-recognized vocational coursework or military training.

The B.S. in applied science and technology, with emphasis in computer science and technology, addresses the field through a whopping 54-hour major comprised of two parts: a 21-hour theoretical core and a 33-hour concentration in computer science technology. The core addresses basic computer literacy, statistics, technical writing, and higher mathematics; the major consists of 3 hours in data structures, 6 hours in programming, 6 hours in computer architecture and Assembly language, 12 hours in advanced topics (students may choose from a variety of fields including artificial intelligence, database design, operating systems, and software engineering), and 6 hours of electives. An associate's degree is also available in this field.

The B.A. in computer science involves a highly flexible 33-hour major: 12 hours covering basic computer literacy, Assembly language, data structures, and higher mathematics; and 21 hours of elective courses.

In addition, a B.S. in business administration and an A.S. in management are both offered with an emphasis in computer information systems.

Union Institute

440 East McMillan Street
Cincinnati, OH 45206-1925

Accreditation: Regional
Year founded: 1964
Ownership: Nonprofit, independent
Phone: (513) 861 6400 • (800) 486 3116
Fax: (513) 861 0779
Email: admission@tui.edu
Web site: www.tui.edu
Degrees offered: Bachelor of Arts (B.A.) or Bachelor of Science (B.S.) in any field
(template-based)
Doctor of Philosophy (Ph.D.) in any field
(template-based/dissertation or project required)

In 1964, a number of traditional institutions formed a consortium called the Union for Experimenting Colleges and Universities. When the consortium was dissolved, the Institute remained, and began to grant degrees.

The bachelor's programs offered by the Union Institute follow what has become a fairly common template model: students (or, as they're called at Union, "learners") complete degree requirements through a combination of new learning (a minimum of 30 semester hours earned through Union) and appraisal of prior learning (through standardized examinations, life-experience evaluation, professional and military training, and coursework done at other institutions). The major can be in almost any field; learners design a program of study with faculty approval and then work to achieve the goals of that program.

The Ph.D. appears to be the only accredited, individualized, and study-based distance-learning doctoral program in the world. The student chooses a committee of advisors, designs a program of study (which must represent new learning but can include anything from industry projects to published papers to documented aikido lessons), completes the contracted program to the satisfaction of the committee, and finishes off the degree with a Project Demonstrating Excellence (PDE), an original and consequential contribution to the field chosen by the student.

United States Open University

901 Market Street, Suite 410
Wilmington, DE 19801

Accreditation:	Pending (Regional Candidacy)
Year founded:	1998
Ownership:	Nonprofit, independent
Phone:	(302) 778 0300 • (800) 232 7705
Fax:	(302) 429 5953
Email:	info@open.edu
Web site:	www.open.edu
Degrees offered:	Bachelor of Science (B.S.) in computing (coursework-based)
	Bachelor of Science (B.S.) in information technology (coursework-based)
	Master of Science (M.S.) in computing (coursework-based/project and thesis required)

The United States Open University serves as the U.S. branch of the very well known and often-emulated Open University in the United Kingdom. Although this new branch was still in the candidacy phases of regional accreditation at press time, it is widely expected to proceed to full accreditation. For more information, contact the Middle States Association of Colleges and Schools (see chapter 5).

The B.S. in computing is a 120-credit program (one credit seems to be roughly equivalent to one semester hour); the computing major comprises 44 of those credits. Courses are required in object modeling, object-oriented programming, networking, databases, and Java; elective courses are available in message coding, C++ programming, SQL, computational mathematics, and digital telecommunications.

The B.S. in information technology is also a 120-credit program. The flexible 39-credit major involves student-picked courses in fields such as artificial intelligence, Web site development (educational or commercial), speech recognition systems, security, digital telecommunication networks, message coding, neural networks, computer-assisted education, and computer history.

The M.S. in computing involves 40 credits: 32 credits of coursework, and the 8-credit project and dissertation (thesis). Courses are available in a variety of fields, including computer architecture, object-oriented programming, advanced Java programming, project management, user interface design, relational databases, and software engineering.

University of Abertay Dundee

Information and Recruitment Office
Bell Street, Dundee DD1 1HG
United Kingdom

Accreditation:	International (GAAP)
Year founded:	1888
Ownership:	Nonprofit, state
Phone:	+44 (1382) 308 921
Fax:	+44 (1382) 308 081
Email:	iro@abertay.ac.uk
Web site:	www.abertay-dundee.ac.uk
Degrees offered:	Master of Science (M.S.) in computer games technology (coursework-based/thesis or project required) Master of Science (M.S.) in information technology (coursework-based/thesis required)

The University of Abertay Dundee offers several online master's programs through the Scottish Knowledge project (*www.scottishknowledge.com*).

The M.S. in computer games technology is a specialized software engineering program focusing on the development of computer games. The program consists of eight modules (addressing issues such as artificial intelligence, graphics design, and audio) and a comprehensive thesis or project.

The M.S. in information technology is designed to give computing majors and non-majors alike a comprehensive, graduate-level background in computing and information science. The program consists of eight modules (seven compulsory, one elective) and a capstone dissertation (thesis). Modules address networking, knowledge discovery, data mining, software engineering, and closely related fields.

University of Bradford

Student Registry, Postgraduate
Richmond Road
Bradford BD7 1DP
United Kingdom

Accreditation:	International (GAAP)
Year founded:	1957
Ownership:	Nonprofit, state
Phone:	+44 (1274) 233 042
Fax:	+44 (1274) 235 810
Email:	pg-admissions@bradford.ac.uk
Web site:	www.brad.ac.uk
Degrees offered:	Master of Philosophy (M.Phil.) in computing (research-based)
	Master of Philosophy (M.Phil.) in cybernetics (research-based)
	Master of Philosophy (M.Phil.) in electronic imaging and media communications (research-based)
	Doctor of Philosophy (Ph.D.) in computing (research-based)
	Doctor of Philosophy (Ph.D.) in cybernetics (research-based)
	Doctor of Philosophy (Ph.D.) in electronic imaging and media communications (research-based)

The University of Bradford offers research-based programs in the above fields.
At least two weeks of on-campus residency are generally required each year, but
this may be negotiable (particularly in extenuating circumstances, and/or when
the student has identified a clearly adequate "home base" facility for research). The
Master of Philosophy (M.Phil.) is considered a higher degree than a taught master's
(e.g., M.A. or M.S.). The M.Phil. generally takes two or three years; the Ph.D. at
least four.

University of Colorado at Boulder

Center for Advanced Training in Engineering and Computer Science
ECOT 127, CB 435
Boulder, CO 80309-0435

Accreditation:	Regional
Year founded:	1876
Ownership:	Nonprofit, state
Phone:	(303) 492 6331
Fax:	(303) 492 5987
Email:	catecs-info@colorado.edu
Web site:	www.colorado.edu/CATECS
Degrees offered:	Master of Engineering (M.Eng.) in computer science (coursework-based/project required)
	Master of Engineering (M.Eng.) in telecommunications (coursework-based/project optional)
	Master of Science (M.S.) in telecommunications (coursework-based/thesis required)

The University of Colorado at Boulder offers engineering-related master's programs to working adults through videocassettes and television courses. Students take one course per semester, finishing the degree in three-and-a-half to five years.

The 30-semester-hour M.Eng. in computer science can be focused on artificial intelligence, database systems, numerical computation, operating systems, parallel processing, programming languages, software engineering, or theory of computation. A final project is required. The program may be completed entirely off-campus except for the oral defense, which must generally be done on-campus.

The 33–34 hour M.Eng. and 37-hour M.S. programs in telecommunications involve 15 hours of coursework in interdisciplinary telecommunications, a 12-hour "nontechnical" component (which can be focused entirely on computer science if the student so wishes), one 3-hour elective, and a final capstone experience. For the M.Eng., this final capstone experience may consist of an additional elective course or a final project; for the M.S., the final capstone experience must be a 6-hour thesis.

M.Eng. and M.S. programs in electrical engineering (which can be tailored to computer engineering) are also available by distance learning.

University of Denver

University College
2211 South Josephine Street
Denver, CO 80208

Accreditation:	Regional
Year founded:	1864
Ownership:	Nonprofit, independent
Phone:	(303) 871 3155 • (800) 347 2042
Fax:	(303) 871 3303
Email:	ucolinfo@du.edu
Web site:	www.universitycollege.du.edu
Degrees offered:	Master of Computer Information Systems (M.C.I.S.) (coursework-based/project required)
	Master of Telecommunications (M.Tel.) (coursework-based/project required)

Through its University College adult learning program, the University of Denver offers degree and certificate programs through online study.

The Master of Computer Information Systems (M.C.I.S.) is a 57-quarter-hour (38-semester-hour) program with concentrations in database management, software engineering, or technical management. A capstone project or practicum is required. At press time, not all of the required courses were yet available by distance learning, but the school is bringing the remaining courses online and estimates that students will be able to complete their degree requirements in a little over two years by taking two distance classes per quarter.

The Master of Telecommunications (M.Tel.) is a 66-quarter-hour (44-semester-hour) program addressing broad issues in telecommunications and telecommunications management, computer networking, and digital media technologies. A capstone project or practicum is required.

Online certificates are available in geographic information systems, network analysis and design, and telecommunications.

University of Glasgow

Glasgow University Initiative in Distance Education (GUIDE)
22 Western Court
Glasgow G12 8SQ
United Kingdom

Accreditation:	International (GAAP)
Year founded:	1451
Ownership:	Nonprofit, state
Phone:	+44 (141) 330 3870
Fax:	+44 (141) 330 4079
Email:	guide@mis.gla.ac.uk
Web site:	www.gla.ac.uk/Inter/GUIDE
Degrees offered:	Master of Science (M.S.) in digital management and preservation (coursework-based/thesis required)

The University of Glasgow has recently begun to offer distance-learning master's programs and diploma programs through its GUIDE initiative, and is slated to offer a master's in digital management and preservation by the end of 2001. This field is in many respects similar to the U.S. field of knowledge acquisition and data mining.

If the structure of the program is modeled after the residential version, the student will be expected to complete 10 modules (addressing such topics as information auditing, electronic recordkeeping, cataloguing, digitization, and data storage) and a dissertation (master's thesis); the program will likely take two to three years to complete. For the latest details on this highly innovative program, contact the school.

University of Houston

Distance Education
4800 Calhoun Road
Houston, TX 77024

Accreditation:	Regional
Year founded:	1927
Ownership:	Nonprofit, state
Phone:	(281) 395 2810 • (800) 687 8488
Email:	deadvisor@uh.edu
Web site:	www.uh.edu/uhdistance
Degrees offered:	Bachelor of Science (B.S.) in mechanical technology with emphasis in computer drafting and design (coursework-based)
	Master of Science (M.S.) in computer science (coursework-based/thesis required)

The University of Houston offers bachelor's completion and master's programs to students nationwide through two-way interactive television (ITV) technology.

Students applying to the B.S. in mechanical technology must already have earned 56 semester hours or the equivalent from a regionally accredited institution. The curriculum involves a 61-hour major divided into four parts: 18 hours of general technology, 20 hours of mechanical technology, 14 hours of computer design and drafting, and 9 hours of field electives (which may be focused on computer-related coursework). The program is accredited by the Accreditation Board for Engineering and Technology (ABET).

The M.S. in computer science involves 24 semester hours of coursework (eight courses) and a thesis. The curriculum covers computer science theory, software engineering, and computer architecture. The program generally takes about three years to complete.

University of Idaho

Engineering Outreach Program
P.O. Box 441014
Moscow, ID 83844-1014

Accreditation:	Regional
Year founded:	1889
Ownership:	Nonprofit, state
Phone:	(800) 824 2889
Email:	outreach@uidaho.edu
Web site:	www.uidaho.edu/evo
Degrees offered:	Master of Engineering (M.Eng.) or Master of Science (M.S.) in computer engineering (coursework-based)
	Master of Science (M.S.) in computer science (coursework-based/thesis optional)

The University of Idaho offers a number of engineering- and technology-related master's degrees through videocourses (augmented, in many cases, by online study). The master's degree generally takes about five years to complete, although theoretically it can be finished in three.

Both the M.Eng. and M.S. in computer engineering require 30 semester hours of study; the M.Eng. requires ten 3-hour courses, while the M.S. requires eight 3-hour courses and a 6-hour thesis. The curriculum centers around a student-defined, faculty-approved program of study; many courses in hardware-focused computer engineering and software engineering are available.

The M.S. in computer science requires 30 or 36 hours of study (30 hours for the thesis track, 36 for the non-thesis track). The program is centered on a 9-hour core; the remaining credit is earned through an individualized, faculty-approved curriculum.

University of Illinois at Springfield

Department of Management Information Systems
College of Business and Management
Springfield, IL 62794-9243

Accreditation:	Regional
Year founded:	1969
Ownership:	Nonprofit, state
Phone:	(217) 206 6067
Fax:	(217) 206 7543
Email:	admissions@uis.edu
Web site:	misonline.uis.edu
Degrees offered:	Master of Science (M.S.) in management information systems (coursework-based)

The University of Illinois at Springfield has recently begun to offer online degrees—beginning with a bachelor's in liberal studies and the M.S. in management information systems—and seems poised to add new programs to the mix.

The M.S. in management information systems involves 44 semester hours of coursework, including an 8-hour thesis/seminar course. The curriculum is highly structured, with 24 hours of required courses (in fields such as strategic decision support systems, database management, telecommunications) and 12 hours of electives (in fields such as Internet marketing, e-commerce, competitive information systems, and technology management).

University of Illinois at Urbana-Champaign

Office of Continuing Engineering Education
400 Engineering Hall
1308 West Green
Urbana, IL 61801

Accreditation:	Regional
Year founded:	1867
Ownership:	Nonprofit, state
Phone:	(217) 333 6634 • (800) 252 1360
Fax:	(217) 333 0015
Email:	graduate@admissions.uiuc.edu
Web site:	online.cen.uiuc.edu
Degrees offered:	Master of Computer Science (M.C.S.) (coursework-based)

The University of Illinois at Urbana-Champaign offers master's degrees in many engineering- and technology-related fields entirely through online study.

The M.C.S. consists of nine courses; the courses are offered synchronously, generally at a rate of one or two graduate-level courses each semester. Coursework tends to focus on software development issues, computer architecture, and other hands-on areas of study. This program does not require a thesis or culminating project.

An M.S. in electrical engineering (which can be focused, to a certain extent, on computer engineering) is also available through online study, videocourses, or a mix of the two.

University of Kent at Canterbury

The Registry
Canterbury, Kent CT2 7NZ
United Kingdom

Accreditation: International (GAAP)
Year founded: 1965
Ownership: Nonprofit, state
Phone: +44 (1227) 824 040
Fax: +44 (1227) 452 196
Email: graduate-office@ukc.ac.uk
Web site: www.ukc.ac.uk
Degrees offered: Master of Philosophy (M.Phil.) in applied language studies in computing
(research-based)
Master of Philosophy (M.Phil.) in computer science
(research-based)
Doctor of Philosophy (Ph.D.) in applied language studies in computing
(research-based)
Doctor of Philosophy (Ph.D.) in computer science
(research-based)

The University of Kent at Canterbury offers many research-based M.Phil. and
Ph.D. degree programs to students worldwide. The student must choose an institution to act as a satellite research site and generally make yearly visits (usually of four
to six weeks duration) to the Kent campus.

University of London

The Information Centre
Malet Street
London WC1E 7HU
United Kingdom

Accreditation:	International (GAAP)
Year founded:	1836
Ownership:	Nonprofit, state
Phone:	+44 (20) 7862 8360
Fax:	+44 (20) 7862 8358
Email:	enquiries@external.lon.ac.uk
Web site:	www.lon.ac.uk/external
Degrees offered:	Bachelor of Science (B.S.) in computing and information systems (examination-based)
	Bachelor of Science (B.S.) in information systems and management (examination-based)
	Bachelor of Science (B.S.) in mathematics, computing, and statistics (examination-based)
	Master of Philosophy (M.Phil.) in computing and information systems (research-based)
	Doctor of Philosophy (Ph.D.) in computing and information systems (research-based)

The University of London, the world's first external degree provider, offers a wide variety of examination-based bachelor's programs to students worldwide through Sylvan Prometric and other testing services. Students may elect to undertake a testing-only option (which is extremely fast and, at roughly US$2500, fairly inexpensive) or a testing-with-instruction option (whereby students complete correspondence courses to prepare for examinations).

The Bachelor of Science (B.S.) in computing and information systems involves 12 examinations focusing on computational mathematics, software engineering, and databases. Optional examinations dealing with various business-related issues (such as accounting information systems and decision sciences) are also available.

The Bachelor of Science (B.S.) in information systems and management involves 12 examinations focusing largely on organizational management, management information systems, software engineering, statistics, and economics.

Also based on 12 exams, the Bachelor of Science (B.S.) in mathematics, computing, and statistics covers a wide variety of interdisciplinary fields, including stellar mathematics, vectors and matrices, databases, fluid dynamics, combinatorics, topology, and game theory.

The University of London also offers research-based M.Phil. and Ph.D. degrees in computing and information systems, and it would seem possible to negotiate nonresidential research arrangements for these programs.

University of Luton

The Research Centre
The Spires, 2 Adelaide Street
Luton, Bedfordshire LU1 5DU
United Kingdom

Accreditation:	International (GAAP)
Year founded:	1993
Ownership:	Nonprofit, state
Phone:	+44 (15) 8274 3700
Email:	admissions@luton.ac.uk
Web site:	www.luton.ac.uk
Degrees offered:	Master of Philosophy (M.Phil.) in computing (research-based)
	Doctor of Philosophy (Ph.D.) in computing (publication-based or research-based)
	Doctor of Science (Sc.D.) in computing (publication-based)

The University of Luton, a former polytechnic, makes several research degrees available to students worldwide.

An unusual opportunity presents itself in the form of Luton's innovative doctorate-by-publication. Individuals who have published extensively in the field of computing may be eligible for a Ph.D. or (for students who already hold a Ph.D. in a computing field) a Sc.D.

The M.Phil. and Ph.D. in computing may also be earned through the more traditional research track. Prospective students should make arrangements with a local university and a local faculty member who is willing to act as an external supervisor. Students are generally expected to spend six weeks on campus at Luton each year, but this policy may be negotiable.

University of Maryland

University College
3501 University Boulevard East
Adelphi, MD 20783

Accreditation: Regional
Year founded: 1856
Ownership: Nonprofit, state
Phone: (301) 985 7000 • (800) 888 8682
Fax: (301) 454 0399
Email: umucinfo@umuc.edu
Web site: www.umuc.edu
Degrees offered: Bachelor of Science (B.S.) in computer and information science
(coursework-based)
Bachelor of Science (B.S.) in computer studies
(coursework-based)
Bachelor of Science (B.S.) in information systems management
(coursework-based)
Master of Science (M.S.) in computer systems management
(coursework-based/project optional)
Master of Science (M.S.) in electronic commerce
(coursework-based/project required)
Master of Science (M.S.) in information technology
(coursework-based)
Master of Science (M.S.) in telecommunications management
(coursework-based/project optional)
Master of Software Engineering (M.Sw.E.)
(coursework-based/project required)

University College, the continuing higher education campus of the University
of Maryland system, offers online bachelor's and master's degrees in a vast array
of fields.

The B.S. in computer and information science involves a 24-semester-hour major
consisting of 12 hours of core courses (C++, computational discrete mathematics,
data structures, and computer architecture), a 9-hour breadth requirement (three of
the following: database systems, languages and systems, networking and distributed
systems, or software engineering), and a 3-hour elective course.

The B.S. in computer studies involves a 24-hour major, which may consist of any
available computer-related courses relevant to a cohesive plan of study.

The B.S. in information systems management, also a 24-hour major, centers on
high-level programming languages, software and hardware concepts, and information systems in organizations. Distributive requirements cover database management, systems analysis, and workplace resource management.

The 33-hour M.S. in computer systems management focuses on issues such as
engineering economics, strategic management of technology, and productivity
management. Specialization tracks are available in applied computer systems,

database systems and security, information resources management, and software development management.

The M.S. in electronic commerce, a 36-hour program, addresses such topics as information risk assessment, e-marketing, social/legal/ethical/regulatory issues, and e-commerce financial management. A 3-hour capstone project is required.

The core of the 33-hour M.S. in information technology examines software-intensive systems, data communications, and systems engineering. In the 12 hours of elective courses, the student can specialize in computer systems, databases, information technology management, software systems, or telecommunications.

The M.S. in telecommunications management is a 39-hour program addressing strategic management of technology and innovation, engineering economics, and other issues related to telecommunications management. Nine hours of depth courses in IT-related telecommunications looks at hardware and software acquisition, network management and design, and systems integration. Students wrap up the program with a 6-hour capstone management project or 6 hours of elective coursework.

The Master of Software Engineering requires 36 semester hours of study. After 24 hours of core courses (addressing project management, software standards, systems development, and a variety of other topics) and 9 hours of electives (chosen from fields such as human resource issues in technology-based organizations, data communications systems, software reliability and reusability, information risk assessment and security management, and strategic management of technology and innovation), students undertake a 3-hour capstone project.

University of Massachusetts at Amherst

Video Instructional Program (VIP)
College of Engineering
Marcus Hall, Box 35115
Amherst, MA 01003-5115

Accreditation:	Regional
Year founded:	1863
Ownership:	Nonprofit, state
Phone:	(413) 545 0063
Fax:	(413) 545 1227
Email:	vip@vip.ecs.umass.edu
Web site:	www.ecs.umass.edu/vip
Degrees offered:	Master of Science (M.S.) in computer science (coursework-based)
	Master of Science (M.S.) in electrical and computer engineering (coursework-based/thesis optional)

The University of Massachusetts at Amherst offers some master's degrees through distance learning via the Video Instruction Program (VIP), whereby students watch videotaped lectures and complete assignments completely off-campus. This program is available to students nationwide, and tailored to the needs of working engineers.

The M.S. in computer science is a 30-semester-hour program focusing on practical issues in the field. This program does not require a thesis or project. The 15-hour core addresses hardware, software, hardware-software interaction, and theory; elective offerings include artificial intelligence and software engineering.

The M.S. in electrical and computer engineering involves 24 (thesis option) or 33 (non-thesis option) hours of coursework. The program centers on a student-defined, faculty-approved program of study that is based on available videocourses. Particularly strong course offerings are available in signal processing, microwave electronics, and software systems.

University of Massachusetts at Lowell

1 University Avenue
Lowell, MA 01854

Accreditation:	Regional
Year founded:	1894
Ownership:	Nonprofit, state
Phone:	(978) 934 2467 • (800) 480 3190
Fax:	(978) 934 3087
Email:	cybered@uml.edu
Web site:	cybered.uml.edu
Degrees offered:	Associate of Science (A.S.) or Bachelor of Science (B.S.) in information systems (coursework-based)

The University of Massachusetts at Lowell offers entire associate's and bachelor's programs in an array of fields entirely through online study.

The A.S. and B.S. in information systems are fairly flexible programs of study focusing primarily on computing and business information systems. Courses are available in multimedia, networking and Internet technologies (e-commerce, Web site development, Flash!, TCP/IP, LAN/WAN), and a variety of programming languages (C, C++, Visual C++, Unix scripting, HTML, Java, JavaScript, Perl, and Visual Basic).

Online certificate programs are also available in information systems, intranet technology, multimedia applications, online communication skills, and Unix.

University of Melbourne

Graduate Centre
Grattan Street
Melbourne 3010
Australia

Accreditation:	International (GAAP)
Year founded:	1989
Ownership:	Nonprofit, state
Phone:	+61 (3) 8344 8670
Email:	j.gilbert@sgs.unimelb.edu.au
Web site:	www.research.unimelb.edu.au
Degrees offered:	Master of Philosophy (M.Phil.) or Doctor of Philosophy (Ph.D.) in computer applications in the social sciences and humanities (research-based)
	Master of Philosophy (M.Phil.) or Doctor of Philosophy (Ph.D.) in computer-assisted language learning (research-based)
	Master of Philosophy (M.Phil.) or Doctor of Philosophy (Ph.D.) in computer education (research-based)
	Master of Philosophy (M.Phil.) or Doctor of Philosophy (Ph.D.) in computer science (research-based)
	Master of Philosophy (M.Phil.) or Doctor of Philosophy (Ph.D.) in information systems (research-based)
	Master of Philosophy (M.Phil.) or Doctor of Philosophy (Ph.D.) in media arts (research-based)
	Master of Philosophy (M.Phil.) or Doctor of Philosophy (Ph.D.) in software engineering (research-based)

The University of Melbourne offers the above programs through off-campus arrangements. Remote students must find a suitable nearby university or medical school research facility and a suitable supervisor in the relevant field(s) of study. The Ph.D. requires at least one year of supervised full-time research (or two years of supervised part-time research) at this remote facility, and generally takes four to six years altogether (the Australian dissertation tends to hover around 100,000 words).

The list of colleges approved as remote facilities is large and growing; students who do not live near an approved site may petition to have their nearby site added to the list of approved schools. Common sense would logically dictate one's success rate; for example, a petition to study for a Ph.D. in software engineering at a community college would probably not be feasible, while a petition to study for a Ph.D. in computer science through a major state university computer science department would probably be accepted with no serious controversy at all.

University of New England

Armidale, NSW 2351
Australia

Accreditation:	International (GAAP)
Year founded:	1938
Ownership:	Nonprofit, state
Phone:	+61 (2) 6773 3333
Fax:	+61 (2) 6773 3122
Email:	ipo@metz.une.edu.au
Web site:	www.une.edu.au
Degrees offered:	Master of Computer Studies (M.C.S.) (coursework-based/thesis optional)
	Master of Science (M.S.) in computer science (research-based)
	Doctor of Philosophy (Ph.D.) in computer science (research-based)

This school offers a truly vast number of bachelor's and master's degrees, as well as research doctorates, to students worldwide. Learning takes place via printed correspondence texts, audio- and videotapes, radio and television broadcasts, and Internet-based study. UNE is Australia's oldest distance education provider, and has over 10,000 students enrolled in external programs.

The M.C.S. consists of nine to ten modules: either nine intensive applied modules (in fields such as advanced parallel computing, advanced databases, advanced networks, multimedia technology, and data mining), or six theory modules plus four applied modules. A thesis may be substituted for two theory modules. The program generally takes 12–18 months for full-time students, or four years for part-time students. This program can be completed entirely by distance learning with no on-campus residency.

The M.S. and Ph.D. programs in computer science are both research-based; the M.S. involves a dissertation of about 45,000 words and takes two to four years to complete, while the Ph.D. involves a dissertation of about 100,000 words and takes four to six years to complete. Primary research interests of the university are in distributed artificial intelligence, information systems, language semantics, multimedia, and parallel and distributed computing. On-campus residency requirements vary considerably depending on the nature of the research conducted, the strength of the student's "home base," and extenuating circumstances. It is our understanding that it may be possible, under certain circumstances, to complete a research degree with no on-campus residency at all.

University of Oregon

AIM Program
18640 NW Walker Road, Suite 1007
Beaverton, OR 97006-8927

Accreditation:	Regional
Year founded:	1876
Ownership:	Nonprofit, state
Phone:	(541) 346 3537 • (800) 824 2714
Fax:	(503) 725 3067
Email:	aim@continue.uoregon.edu
Web site:	aim.uoregon.edu
Degrees offered:	Master of Science (M.S.) in applied information management (coursework-based/research paper required)

The University of Oregon offers an M.S. in applied information management that can be completed entirely through online study.

This 54-credit program is comprised of four parts: 12 credits of information management (data management and communications, information systems and management, and project management), 12 credits of business management (business solutions with technology, management of organizations, and marketing management and planning), 12 credits of information design, and 12 credits of applied research (two research courses and a capstone research paper). Remaining credit requirements are fulfilled through elective coursework.

University of Phoenix Online

3157 East Elwood Street
Phoenix, AZ 85034

Accreditation:	Regional
Year founded:	1976
Ownership:	Proprietary
Phone:	(602) 387 7000 • (800) 366 9699
Fax:	(602) 387 6440
Web site:	online.uophx.edu
Degrees offered:	Bachelor of Science (B.S.) in business and information systems (coursework-based)
	Master of Science (M.S.) in computer information systems (coursework-based)

The University of Phoenix Online offers a number of degree programs entirely through online study.

The B.S. in business information systems involves a 48-semester-hour major; 12 hours focus on business, the other 36 on information systems. The information systems component is comprised of 15 hours of core coursework and a 21-hour specialization in one of the following fields: business systems analysis, database management, network and telecommunications, programming and Web management, or operating systems.

The M.S. in computer information systems is a 45-hour program addressing a variety of subjects related to networking, business information systems, and software engineering; this program is fairly flexible and can be tailored to specific student interests. No thesis or project is required.

An MBA with emphasis in technology management is also available.

University of South Africa

P.O. Box 392
Unisa 0003
South Africa

Accreditation: International (GAAP)
Year founded: 1873
Ownership: Nonprofit, state
Phone: +27 (12) 429 3111
Fax: +27 (12) 429 3221
Email: study-info@unisa.ac.za
Web site: www.unisa.ac.za
Degrees offered: Bachelor of Commerce (B.Com.) in informatics
(coursework-based)
Bachelor of Science (B.S.) in computer science
(coursework-based)
Bachelor of Science (B.S.) in information systems
(coursework-based)
Honours Bachelor of Science (Hons B.S.) in computer science
(coursework-based)
Honours Bachelor of Science (Hons B.S.) in information systems
(coursework-based)
Master of Science (M.S.) in computer science
(research-based or coursework-based/thesis required)
Master of Science (M.S.) in information systems
(research-based or coursework-based/thesis required)
Doctor of Philosophy (Ph.D.) in computer science
(research-based)

The University of South Africa offers a vast number of programs at all levels in a variety of fields, and all of the programs listed above may be completed entirely by distance learning with no on-campus residency whatsoever. Instruction for the coursework-based programs takes place mainly by correspondence, supplemented by proctored examinations.

Each of the standard bachelor's degrees listed above consists of 32 highly rigorous correspondence courses. The informatics curriculum focuses primarily on business information systems, the computer science program (available with an optional specialization in artificial intelligence) focuses primarily on computer science theory and software engineering, and the information systems curriculum represents a blend of business computing, traditional computer science, and information science.

Please note that the standard South African bachelor's degree is a three-year program rather than a four-year program; the Honours bachelor's involves one to two additional years of study and is regarded as a graduate-level credential.

The master's degrees described above may be completed through a coursework-and-thesis track (wherein students complete five rigorous modules in the field and a culminating thesis) or through a research-only track (wherein students undertake an original supervised dissertation of significant length and publishable quality).

The Ph.D. in computer science, following the standard Commonwealth format, involves guided research and culminates in a dissertation that must represent an original contribution to the field.

In the United States, the University of South Africa is represented by the American International Higher Education Corporation. Prospective U.S. students interested in any of the above programs should contact this agency, which may be reached at AIHEC, 5808 Misty Hill Cove, Austin, TX 78759; phone: (512) 343 2031; fax: (512) 343 8644; email: *jcraparo@aihec.com*; Web site: *www.aihec.com*.

University of South Australia

International Programs
G.P.O. Box 2471
Adelaide SA 5001
Australia

Accreditation:	International (GAAP)
Year founded:	1991
Ownership:	Nonprofit, state
Phone:	+61 (8) 8302 0114
Fax:	+61 (8) 8302 0233
Email:	international.office@unisa.edu.au
Web site:	www.unisa.edu.au
Degrees offered:	Bachelor of Arts (B.A.) in communication and media management (coursework-based)
	Bachelor of Computer and Information Science (B.C.I.S.) (coursework-based)
	Master of Arts (M.A.) in communication management (coursework-based)

The University of South Australia offers programs at all levels by correspondence to students worldwide.

The Bachelor of Arts (B.A.) in communication and media management is in many respects a telecommunications management program, if a somewhat broad version. Modules deal with media studies, advertising, and rhetoric in addition to Internet and digital media technology.

The Bachelor of Computer and Information Science (B.C.I.S.) is a cutting-edge program focusing on Java programming, telecommunications, e-commerce, databases, and software engineering.

The Master of Arts (M.A.) in communication management addresses a broad range of communications-related disciplines, but may be focused on Internet communications and digital media technology. Students are required to complete six modules; although no thesis is required, the writing assignments involved with each module are significant.

In addition to the programs described here, further distance-learning opportunities are available to Australian citizens.

University of Southern California

USC Distance Education Network (DEN)
3650 McClintock Avenue, OHE 108
Los Angeles, CA 90089-1455

Accreditation: Regional
Year founded: 1880
Ownership: Nonprofit, independent
Phone: (213) 821 1321 • (877) 740 1336
Fax: (213) 821 0851
Email: webclass@usc.edu
Web site: den.usc.edu
Degrees offered: Master of Science (M.S.) in computer engineering
(coursework-based/thesis optional)
Master of Science (M.S.) in computer science
(coursework-based/thesis optional)
Master of Science (M.S.) in systems architecting and engineering
(coursework-based/thesis optional)

The University of Southern California offers entire degree programs online through its Distance Education Network (DEN) program.

The 27-semester-hour M.S. in computer engineering consists of 6 hours of core courses addressing computer systems architecture and VLSI design; a 12-hour concentration in computer-aided design, computer architecture, networks, or VLSI; and 9 hours of electives.

The M.S. in computer science can be completed through a general track (consisting of a 21-hour core and 6 hours of electives for a total of 27 hours) or a specialization track (consisting of a 9-hour core and a 24-hour specialization for a total of 33 hours). Specializations are available in computer networking, multimedia and creative technology, robotics and automation, and software engineering.

The M.S. in systems architecting and engineering involves 30 hours of study: 9 hours in technology management, 9 hours in general engineering and technology, and a 12-hour specialization in one of ten possible fields, six of which are computer related: artificial intelligence and neural networks, automation and control systems, communication and signal processing systems, computer and information systems, integrated media systems, and software process architecting.

University of Southern Queensland

International Office
Toowoomba QLD 4350
Australia

Accreditation:	International (GAAP)
Year founded:	1967
Ownership:	Nonprofit, state
Phone:	+61 (74) 631 2362
Fax:	+61 (74) 636 2211
Email:	international@usq.edu.au
Web site:	www.usq.edu.au
Degrees offered:	Bachelor of Business (B.Bus.) in information technology management (coursework-based)
	Bachelor of Information Technology (coursework-based)
	Master of Business (M.Bus.) in information systems (coursework-based/thesis required)
	Master of Business Information Technology (coursework-based/project required/thesis optional)
	Master of e-Business (coursework-based/project optional)
	Master of Engineering (M.Eng.) in computer systems engineering (research-based/project-based)
	Master of Engineering Technology in computer systems engineering technology (coursework-based/thesis and project required)
	Master of Geomatics (research-based/project based)
	Master of Information Technology (coursework-based/thesis required)
	Master of Professional Computing (coursework-based/project optional)

Formerly known as the Darling Downs Institute of Advanced Education, the University of Southern Queensland offers degrees in a truly vast array of fields, and new programs are constantly being developed. Courses are available by correspondence (supplemented by other media) and, increasingly, online study.

The B.Bus. in information technology management consists of 16 units: 8 core units in business and 8 major units in information technology management (addressing such fields as knowledge-based systems, Oracle databases, systems analysis, business information programming, and systems security). As 2 of the compulsory courses are in computer-related fields, 10 of the 16 total modules can be focused on IT issues.

The Bachelor of Information Technology consists of 8 core modules and a specialization in computer software development (12 modules addressing topics such as systems analysis, Java, COBOL, Visual Basic, Oracle databases, and networking) or information technology management (8 modules addressing topics such as business programming, computer security, knowledge-based systems, systems analysis, and Oracle databases). The program generally takes about six years to complete.

The M.Bus. in information systems involves 5 business courses and a thesis in information systems; some short residencies may be required.

The Master of Business Information Technology consists of 9 modules, a project, and an optional thesis. Seven modules are compulsory and 2 are elective.

The M.Eng. in computer systems engineering consists of 12 directed research projects. Distance students will need to demonstrate that adequate facilities are locally available to conduct the relevant research, and it may be necessary for a supervisor to visit the student's site.

The online Master of e-Business consists of 12 units in fields such as Web publishing, Java, decision support systems, and computer security. Students may choose to undertake a project in lieu of 2 units.

For the Master of Engineering Technology in computer systems engineering technology, another 12-module program, a joint thesis/project is required.

Like the M.Eng., the Master of Geomatics consists of 12 directed research projects, and distance students must have access to adequate research facilities.

The Master of Information Technology consists of 4–6 modules and a thesis. Students choose 4 or 5 modules in information technology and, optionally, one course in a secondary field (such as applied mathematics or management). The program takes about four years to complete. The thesis/dissertation in this program generally requires a short residency.

The Master of Professional Computing consists of 12 units organized around an individualized, faculty-approved program of study. Students may choose to undertake a project in lieu of 2 modules.

A bachelor's degree in communication and media study and master's degrees in educational technology, health communication, and online learning are also available, as are a vast array of certificate and graduate diploma programs in all of the fields listed here.

University of Strathclyde

International Office
Level 4, Graham Hills Building
50 George Street
Glasgow G1 1QE
United Kingdom

Accreditation:	International (GAAP)
Year founded:	1796
Ownership:	Nonprofit, state
Phone:	+44 (141) 548 3291
Fax:	+44 (141) 553 1546
Email:	international@mis.strath.ac.uk
Web site:	itlaw.law.strath.ac.uk
Degrees offered:	Master of Laws (LL.M.) in information technology law (coursework-based/thesis required)

The University of Strathclyde offers an innovative LL.M. in information technology law entirely through online study, with no residency required.

Students must complete four modules (in fields such as e-commerce law, information security, intellectual property, liability for defective software, and telecommunications law) and an approved dissertation of 15,000 to 20,000 words. The program generally takes about two years to complete.

Although the LL.M. is generally considered a post-professional (e.g., post-J.D. or LL.B.) credential, other applicants with a strong academic or professional background in the field of information technology may be considered.

University of Tasmania

Board of Graduate Studies by Research
Churchill Avenue, Sandy Bay
G.P.O. Box 252-45
Hobart, Tasmania 7001
Australia

Accreditation:	International (GAAP)
Year founded:	1890
Ownership:	Nonprofit, state
Phone:	+61 (3) 6226 2762
Fax:	+61 (3) 6226 7497
Email:	international.office@utas.edu.au
Web site:	www.international.utas.edu.au
Degrees offered:	Master of Philosophy (M.Phil.) in computing (research-based or publication-based)
	Master of Philosophy (M.Phil.) in information systems (research-based or publication-based)
	Doctor of Philosophy (Ph.D.) in computing (research-based or publication-based)
	Doctor of Philosophy (Ph.D.) in information systems (research-based or publication-based)

The University of Tasmania offers research-based programs to students worldwide. Study takes place largely off-campus, augmented by negotiated yearly residencies.

The degrees can also be earned based on prior written work (published or unpublished); students will need to write an integrative paper explaining the work and its contribution (or potential contribution) to the field.

University of Technology, Sydney

P.O. Box 123
Broadway, NSW 2007
Australia

Accreditation: International (GAAP)
Year founded: 1965
Ownership: Nonprofit, state
Phone: +61 (2) 9514 2000
Email: info.office@uts.edu.au
Web site: www.gradschool.uts.edu.au/courses/phdpub_info.html
Degrees offered: Doctor of Philosophy (Ph.D.) in computer science
(publication-based)
Doctor of Philosophy (Ph.D.) in computer systems engineering
(publication-based)
Doctor of Philosophy (Ph.D.) in information studies
(publication-based)
Doctor of Philosophy (Ph.D.) in information systems
(publication-based)
Doctor of Philosophy (Ph.D.) in media arts
(publication-based)
Doctor of Philosophy (Ph.D.) in telecommunications engineering
(publication-based)

The Ph.D.-by-publication program awards doctoral degrees to established researchers on the basis of their record of academic publication and their original scholarly contribution to knowledge. An applicant must submit his or her published works and an extended paper integrating the work and highlighting its value to the field.

In Australian doctorate-by-publication programs, the integrating paper itself can sometimes be quite lengthy; we have heard one story of such a paper that exceeded 100,000 words (the length of an average Australian Ph.D. dissertation).

University of Teesside

Research Office
Middlesbrough, Cleveland TS1 3BA
United Kingdom

Accreditation:	International (GAAP)
Year founded:	1929
Ownership:	Nonprofit, state
Phone:	+44 (1642) 384 408
Email:	k.ludlow@tees.ac.uk
Web site:	www.tees.ac.uk
Degrees offered:	Master of Philosophy (M.Phil.) in computing and media (research-based or publication-based)
	Doctor of Philosophy (Ph.D.) in computing and media (research-based or publication-based)

The University of Teesside offers research-based degree programs to students worldwide, and it is possible to complete these programs largely off-campus. The student will need to secure local facilities for research and ensure reliable means of contact between the student and supervisor (mentor); beyond this, residency is negotiable.

It may also be possible to negotiate a research degree based on prior publication; the student will need to write an integrative work demonstrating the manner in which the published writings have contributed to the student's field of study.

University of Tennessee at Knoxville

The School of Information Sciences
804 Volunteer Boulevard
Knoxville, TN 37996-4330

Accreditation:	Regional
Year founded:	1794
Ownership:	Nonprofit, state
Phone:	(865) 974 2858
Fax:	(865) 974 4967
Email:	disteducation@utk.edu
Web site:	www.outreach.utk.edu
Degrees offered:	Master of Science (M.S.) in information sciences (coursework-based/thesis optional)

The University of Tennessee at Knoxville offers an M.S. in information sciences almost entirely by online study; a one-week orientation session is the only required residency. This program is accredited by the American Library Association (ALA).

The program involves 42 semester hours of coursework: a 15-hour core (addressing information access and retrieval, information technologies, and information content representation) and a 27-hour individualized, faculty-approved specialization, which can be tailored to a variety of computer-related fields, such as Web page design or online information retrieval.

University of Texas

Office of Information Technology and Distance Education
201 West 7th Street
Austin, TX 78701

Accreditation:	Regional
Year founded:	1973
Ownership:	Nonprofit, state
Phone:	(512) 499 4207 • (888) 839 2716
Email:	telecampus@utsystem.edu
Web site:	www.telecampus.utsystem.edu
Degrees offered:	Master of Science (M.S.) in computer science (coursework-based/thesis or project optional)
	Master of Science (M.S.) in computer science and engineering (coursework-based/thesis required, project optional)

The University of Texas Telecampus offers master's degrees in many fields entirely through online study, with no on-campus attendance required. The M.S. in computer science is awarded by the University of Texas at Dallas, while the M.S. in computer science and engineering is awarded by the University of Texas at Arlington.

The M.S. in computer science involves 27 to 33 hours of coursework and a 6-hour thesis. The general track explores operating systems, networking, compiler construction, databases, and programming language design. Students may opt to specialize in networking and telecommunications or software engineering.

The M.S. in computer science and engineering involves 31 hours of coursework, including a 6-hour thesis. Students may design an individualized track or specialize in any of the following pre-designed tracks: artificial intelligence, databases, graphics and image processing, software engineering, systems and architecture, or theory and algorithms.

University of Wales—Aberystwyth

Old College
King Street
Aberystwyth, Ceredigion SY23 2AX
United Kingdom

Accreditation:	International (GAAP)
Year founded:	1872
Ownership:	Nonprofit, state
Phone:	+44 (1970) 622 090
Fax:	+44 (1970) 622 921
Email:	cs-pg-admissions@aber.ac.uk
Web site:	www.aber.ac.uk
Degrees offered:	Master of Philosophy (M.Phil.) in computer science (research-based)
	Doctor of Philosophy (Ph.D.) in computer science (research-based)

The Aberystwyth campus of the University of Wales system offers M.Phil. and Ph.D. degrees that can be studied on a part-time basis, with students traveling to Wales for a couple of weeks each year, or handled full-time through a suitable academic center or place of employment.

The primary research interests of the computer science department are computational biology (focusing on "innovative machine learning and chemometrics for data mining and data interpretation"), intelligent robotics (focusing on mobile robots, robot kinematics, tactile function, and a particularly interesting research project in modeling intelligent kinematic models of the human skeleton), model-based systems (including a fascinating interdisciplinary program in qualitative biological systems analysis), and software engineering (addressing networking/distributed systems, object-oriented programming, artificial intelligence engineering, software industry issues, and other relevant topics).

University of Wisconsin at Madison

Department of Engineering Professional Development
432 North Lake Street
Madison, WI 53706

Accreditation:	Regional
Year founded:	1849
Ownership:	Nonprofit, state
Phone:	(800) 462 0876
Fax:	(608) 263 3160
Email:	custserv@engr.wisc.edu
Web site:	epdweb.engr.wisc.edu
Degrees offered:	Master of Science (M.S.) in electrical and computer engineering (coursework-based)

The M.S. in electrical and computer engineering (with emphasis in power systems) can be completed almost entirely through a mix of Internet study, videocourses, and audio lectures. This 33-semester-hour program requires a thesis or project.

It is also possible to complete a considerable amount of the M.S. in computational science through distance learning; contact the school for details.

University of Wisconsin at Superior

Extended Degree Program
Erlanson 105, P.O. Box 2000
Superior, WI 54880

Accreditation:	Regional
Year founded:	1893
Ownership:	Nonprofit, state
Phone:	(715) 394 8487
Fax:	(715) 394 8139
Email:	extdegree@uwsuperior.edu
Web site:	edp.uwsuper.edu
Degrees offered:	Bachelor of Science (B.S.) in any field (template-based)

The external B.S. can be earned entirely off-campus, through a mix of college coursework, prior learning (transfer credit, standardized examinations, or life-experience evaluation), and faculty-guided independent study. The individualized major is 54–57 semester hours, and Superior's faculty can accommodate many computer-related fields of study.

Upper Iowa University

External Degree
P.O. Box 1861
Fayette, IA 52142

Accreditation:	Regional
Year founded:	1857
Ownership:	Nonprofit, independent
Phone:	(319) 425 5252 • (888) 877 3742
Fax:	(319) 425 5353
Email:	extdegree@uiu.edu
Web site:	www.uiu.edu
Degrees offered:	Bachelor of Science (B.S.) in technology and information management (coursework-based)

Upper Iowa University offers several associate's and bachelor's degree programs through its External Degree Program (EDP). Credit is earned primarily through online study, although some general requirements may be fulfilled through transfer credit, correspondence, or standardized examinations.

The B.S. in technology and information management involves 120 semester hours of coursework: a 66-hour major (comprised of 45 hours of business courses and 21 hours of IT courses) and at least 54 hours of general education and elective coursework.

The 21-hour IT component addresses computer programming, networking, MCSE certification track courses, telecommunications, project management, and databases. The curriculum is tightly structured and addresses all relevant issues in IT management in a survey fashion.

Appendix A: Online and Correspondence Courses

The following regionally accredited schools offer courses in computer-related fields. This might come in handy for any of several reasons:

If you're considering a graduate program but don't hold an undergraduate degree in a computer-related field, you can take individual courses to bolster your credentials.

Almost every program described in this book will accept a limited amount of transfer credit in some form or another, and a few (such as Excelsior College and Thomas Edison State College) will actually accept an unlimited amount of transfer credit from other accredited schools.

If you want to give distance learning a "test drive" before committing to an entire degree program, taking one or two distance-learning courses might be a good way to decide if this approach is for you.

For details (including costs, delivery method, and requirements), contact the schools directly.

Arizona State University
Extended Campus
P.O. Box 871708
Tempe, AZ 85287-1708
Phone: (480) 965 3986
Email: xed@asu.edu
Web site: www.asu.edu/xed

Courses in a variety of computer-related fields, most notably telecommunications and management information systems.

Boise State University
Extended Studies
1910 University Drive
Boise, ID 83725
Phone: (208) 426 1966
Email: htubbs@boisestate.edu
Web site: www.boisestate.edu

Graduate courses in educational technology, and undergraduate courses in a variety of computer-related fields.

Carnegie Mellon University
School of Computer Science – ISRI
5000 Forbes Avenue
Pittsburgh, PA 15213-3891
Phone: (412) 268 1593
Fax: (412) 268 5413
Email: distance-info@cs.cmu.edu
Web site: www.cmu.edu

Graduate courses in software engineering and information resource management.

Colorado State University
Division of Educational Outreach
Spruce Hall
Fort Collins, CO 80523-1040
Phone: (970) 491 5288 • (800) 525 4950
Fax: (970) 491 7885
Email: questions@learn.colostate.edu
Web site: www.colostate.edu

Undergraduate and graduate courses in computer science, computer engineering, telecommunications, and related fields.

Florida State University
Office of Distributed and Distance Learning
University Center, Suite C3500
Tallahassee, FL 32306-2540
Phone: (850) 645 0393 • (877) 357 8283
Email: students@oddl.fsu.edu
Web site: www.oddl.fsu.edu

Undergraduate courses in computer science and software applications.

Illinois Institute of Technology
IITV
10 West 31st Street, 226 SB
Chicago, IL 60616
Phone: (312) 567 3167
Fax: (312) 567 5913
Email: hewitt@iit.edu
Web site: www.iit-online.iit.edu

Undergraduate courses in computer science and software applications; graduate offerings are being expanded.

Indiana University
School of Continuing Studies
Owen Hall 001
Bloomington, IN 47405
Phone: (812) 855 8995
Fax: (812) 855 8997
Email: scs@indiana.edu
Web site: scs.indiana.edu

Undergraduate courses in computer information systems and software applications; graduate courses in technology management.

Johns Hopkins University
Department of Computer Science
3400 North Charles Street
Baltimore, MD 21218
Phone: (410) 516 8775
Fax: (410) 516 6134
Email: gotojhu@jhu.edu
Web site: www.jhu.edu

Courses in computer science and computer engineering.

Kansas State University
13 College Court
Manhattan, KS 66506
Phone: (785) 532 5686 • (800) 622 2578
Fax: (785) 532 5637
Email: info@dce.ksu.edu
Web site: www.dce.ksu.edu

Undergraduate courses in several computer-related fields, and graduate-level courses in software engineering.

Lamar University
4400 Martin Luther King Boulevard
Beaumont, TX 77710
Phone: (409) 880 8775
Email: csdept@hal.lamar.edu
Web site: www.lamar.edu

Courses in computer engineering, computer science, and software applications.

Marshall University
400 Hal Green Boulevard
Huntington, WV 25755
Phone: (304) 696 3160
Email: cite@marshall.edu
Web site: www.marshall.edu

Courses in computer information systems and technology management.

Michigan State University
Outreach Instructional Programs
51 Kellogg Center
East Lansing, MI 48824-1022
Phone: (517) 353 0791 • (877) 468 6678
Fax: (517) 432 1327
Email: gotomsu@msu.edu
Web site: vu.msu.edu

Courses in computer engineering, computer information systems, and telecommunications.

Mississippi State University
Office of Admissions
P.O. Box 6305
Mississippi State, MS 39762
Phone: (662) 325 2224
Fax: (662) 325 7360
Email: msuinfo@ur.msstate.edu
Web site: www.msstate.edu

Courses at all levels in computer engineering and computer science.

Montana State University
Office of Admissions
P.O. Box 172180
Bozeman, MT 59717-2180
Phone: (406) 994 6617
Email: csinfo@cs.montana.edu
Web site: www.montana.edu

Undergraduate courses in computer engineering, computer science, and software engineering; graduate courses in educational technology.

New York University
Office of Admissions
22 Washington Square North
New York, NY 10011-9191
Phone: (212) 998 1212
Email: admissions@cs.nyu.edu
Web site: www.nyu.edu

Courses in computer science and educational technology.

Northeastern University
Office of Undergraduate Admissions
360 Huntington Avenue, 150 Richards Hall
Boston, MA 02115
Phone: (617) 373 2462
Fax: (617) 373 5121
Email: undergradschool@ccs.neu.edu
Web site: www.northeastern.edu

Courses in computer engineering technology and computer science.

Oklahoma State University
Center for Academic Services
324 Student Union
Stillwater, OK 74078-1012
Phone: (405) 744 5668
Fax: (405) 744 9097
Email: admit@okstate.edu
Web site: osu.okstate.edu

Graduate courses in computer engineering; undergraduate courses in a variety of computer-related fields.

Old Dominion University
Office of Distance Learning and Extended
  Education
Gornto TELETECHNET Center, 4th Floor
Norfolk, VA 23529
Phone: (757) 683 3163 • (800) 968 2638
Fax: (757) 683 5492
Email: admit@odu.edu
Web site: web.odu.edu

Courses in computer science and management information systems.

Oregon State University
Distance and Continuing Education
4943 The Valley Library
Corvallis, OR 97331-4504
Phone: (541) 737 2676 • (800) 235 6559
Fax: (541) 737 2734
Email: ostateu@orst.edu
Web site: statewide.orst.edu

Courses in computer science and history of technology.

St. Leo University
33701 State Road 52
Saint Leo, FL 33574
Phone: (352) 588 8283
Web site: www.saintleo.edu

Courses in computer information systems and management information systems.

Skidmore College
University Without Walls
815 North Broadway
Saratoga Springs, NY 12866
Phone: (518) 580 5450
Fax: (518) 580 5449
Email: uww@skidmore.edu
Web site: www.skidmore.edu

Courses in business information systems and computer science.

Southern Methodist University
School of Engineering and Applied Science
3145 Dyer Street
Dallas, TX 75205-0338
Phone: (214) 768 3083
Fax: (214) 768 3085
Email: enrolserv@mail.smu.edu
Web site: www.smu.edu

Courses in computer engineering, computer science, and telecommunications.

Stanford University
Stanford Center for Professional Development
496 Lomita Mall, Durand Building, Room 401
Stanford, CA 94305-4036
Phone: (650) 725 3000
Fax: (650) 725 2868
Email: sitn-registration@stanford.edu
Web site: scpd.stanford.edu

Courses in computer science and telecommunications.

State University of New York at Buffalo
Undergraduate Admissions
17 Capen Hall
Box 601660
Buffalo, NY 14260-1660
Phone: (716) 645 2422 • (888) 822 3648
Fax: (716) 645 3656
Email: cse-uginfo@cse.buffalo.edu
Web site: www.buffalo.edu

Courses in computer engineering and computer science.

Strayer University
1025 15th Street NW
Washington, DC 20005
Phone: (703) 339 1850 • (800) 422 8055
Fax: (703) 339 1852
Email: jct@strayer.edu
Web site: www.strayer.edu

Courses in computer science and management information systems.

Texas Tech University
Outreach and Extended Studies
6901 Quaker Avenue
Lubbock, TX 79413
Phone: (806) 742 7200 • (800) 692 6877
Fax: (806) 742 7222
Email: distlearn@ttu.edu
Web site: www.ttu.edu

Graduate-level courses in computer engineering, software engineering, and telecommunications; undergraduate courses in a variety of computer-related fields.

University of Alabama
New College
P.O. Box 870182
Tuscaloosa, AL 35487-0182
Phone: (205) 348 3019
Email: info@exd.ccs.ua.edu
Web site: bama.ua.edu/~exd

Courses in a number of computer-related fields.

University of California—Los Angeles
Department K
UCLA Extension
P.O. Box 24901
Los Angeles, CA 90024-0901
Phone: (310) 825 9971 • (818) 784 7006
Fax: (310) 206 3223
Web site: www.unex.ucla.edu

Courses in a vast array of fields including computer engineering, computer graphics, computer science, management information systems, and telecommunications.

University of Colorado
CATECS, ECOT 127, CB 435
Boulder, CO 80309-0435
Phone: (303) 492 6331
Fax: (303) 492 5987
Email: catecs-info@colorado.edu
Web site: www.colorado.edu/CATECS

Courses in computer engineering, computer science, and software engineering.

University of Florida
Gainesville, FL 32611
Phone: (352) 392 3261
Fax: (352) 392 8791
Web site: www.fcd.ufl.edu

Courses in business information systems and computer science.

University of Houston
Distance Education
4800 Calhoun Road
Houston, TX 77024
Phone: (281) 395 2810 • (800) 687 8488
Email: deadvisor@uh.edu
Web site: www.uh.edu/uhdistance

Courses in computer-aided design, computer engineering, computer science, and educational technology.

University of Idaho
Engineering Outreach Program
P.O. Box 441014
Moscow, ID 83844-1014
Phone: (800) 824 2889
Email: outreach@uidaho.edu
Web site: www.uidaho.edu/evo

Graduate courses in computer engineering, computer science, educational technology, and technology management; undergraduate courses in a variety of computer-related fields.

University of Iowa
Division of Continuing Education
116 International Center
Iowa City, IA 52242-1802
Phone: (319) 335 2575 • (800) 272 6430
Fax: (319) 335 2740
Email: credit-programs@uiowa.edu
Web site: www.uiowa.edu

Courses in computer science and management information systems.

University of Maryland at College Park
College Park, MD 20742
Phone: (301) 405 2672
Fax: (301) 405 6707
Email: ugrad@cs.umd.edu
Web site: www.maryland.edu

Courses in computer engineering, computer science, and telecommunications.

University of Massachusetts at Amherst
Video Instruction Program (VIP)
College of Engineering
Marcus Hall, Box 35115
Amherst, MA 01003-5115
Phone: (413) 545 0063
Fax: (413) 545 1227
Email: vip@vip.ecs.umass.edu
Web site: www.umass.edu

Graduate courses in computer engineering and computer science; undergraduate courses in several computer-related fields.

University of Massachusetts at Lowell
One University Avenue
Lowell, MA 01854
Phone: (978) 934 2467 • (800) 480 3190
Fax: (978) 934 3087
Email: cybered@uml.edu
Web site: cybered.uml.edu

Courses in computer information systems, multimedia, networking, and a variety of other computer-related fields.

University of Minnesota
Minneapolis, MN 55455
Phone: (612) 625 4002
Fax: (612) 625 0572
Email: admissions@umn.edu
Web site: www.umn.edu

Courses in computer engineering, computer science, and software engineering.

University of Missouri at Columbia
Columbia, MO 65211
Phone: (573) 882 2121
Email: gradsec@cecs.missouri.edu
Web site: www.missouri.edu

Courses in computer engineering and computer science.

University of Nebraska at Lincoln
Lincoln, NE 68588
Phone: (402) 472 2401
Fax: (402) 472 7767
Email: info@cse.unl.edu
Web site: www.unl.edu

Courses in computer engineering and computer science.

University of Nebraska at Omaha
6001 Dodge Street
Omaha, NE 68182
Phone: (402) 554 2423
Fax: (402) 554 2289
Email: ugprog@cs.unomaha.edu
Web site: www.unomaha.edu

Courses in computer engineering, computer science, and telecommunications.

University of Oklahoma
College of Liberal Studies
1700 Asp Avenue STE 226
Norman, OH 73072-6400
Phone: (405) 325 1061 • (800) 522 4389
Fax: (405) 325 7132
Email: cls@ou.edu
Web site: www.ou.edu/cls

Courses in computer information systems and management information systems.

University of South Carolina
Engineering and Information Technology
Swearingen Engineering Center
Columbia, SC 29208
Phone: (803) 777 4192
Web site: www.engr.sc.edu/apogee

Graduate courses in computer engineering and computer information systems; undergraduate courses in a variety of information technology fields.

University of Tennessee at Knoxville
Knoxville, TN 37996
Phone: (865) 974 1000
Fax: (865) 974 3536
Email: disteducation@utk.edu
Web site: www.outreach.utk.edu

Graduate courses in data mining and information science; undergraduate courses in many computer-related fields.

University of Tennessee Space Institute
B.H. Goethert Parkway
Tullahoma, TN 37388-9700
Phone: (931) 393 7432
Fax: (931) 393 7346
Email: admit@utsi.edu
Web site: www.utsi.edu

Graduate courses in computer engineering and computer science.

University of Texas
Office of Information Technology and Distance
    Education
201 West 7th Street
Austin, TX 78701
Phone: (512) 499 4207 • (888) 839 2716
Email: telecampus@utsystem.edu
Web site: www.telecampus.utsystem.edu

Graduate courses in computer science and educational technology; undergraduate courses in a variety of computer-related fields.

University of Washington
Office of Admissions
Schmitz Hall, Box 355840
Seattle, WA 98195-5840
Phone: (206) 543 1695
Fax: (206) 543 2969
Email: adkuwadm@u.washington.edu
Web site: www.washington.edu

Courses in computer engineering and computer science.

Utah State University
Independent Study and Distance Education
3080 Old Main Hill
Logan, UT 84322-3080
Phone: (435) 797 2137
Email: de-info@ext.usu.edu
Web site: www.ext.usu.edu

Courses in business information systems, computer science, and educational technology.

Webster University
470 East Lockwood Avenue
St. Louis, MO 63119
Phone: (314) 968 7178
Email: admit@webster.edu
Web site: www.webster.edu

Courses in computer science.

Appendix B: For More Information on Schools in This Book

If you have questions about one of the schools described in this book, don't hesitate to write to us. We'll do our best to help. These are the ground rules:

What to do before writing to us

1. Point your Web browser to *www.degree.net/updates/computerdegrees*. At this site we will post updates and corrections to the school listings in this book.

2. Do your own homework. Check first with your local library, the relevant state education department, or the Better Business Bureau, as well as, of course, searching on the Internet. Any major search engine should locate a school's Web site. There is, for instance, a complete university list in the "universities" section of *www.yahoo.com*.

3. Schools do move, and the post office will only forward mail for a short while. If a letter comes back as "undeliverable," call directory assistance ("information") in the school's city and see if a number is listed. They can give you a new street address as well.

4. Schools do change phone numbers, and the telephone company will only notify you of the new number for a short while. If you can't reach a school by phone, write to it, or try directory information to see if there has been a change.

Writing to us

If you cannot reach a school by phone or mail or on the Internet, if you have new information you think we should know, or if you have questions or problems, then please write and let us know. We may be able to help.

Enclose a self-addressed, stamped envelope. If you are outside the United States, enclose two international postal reply coupons, available at your post office.

If you want extensive advice or opinions on your personal situation, you will need to use the Degree Consulting Service that John established (although he no longer runs it). This service is described in Appendix D.

Don't get too annoyed if we don't respond promptly. We do our best, but we get overwhelmed sometimes, and we travel a lot.

Please don't telephone.

Write to us at:

Best Computer Degrees
Degree.net
P.O. Box 7123
Berkeley, CA 94707 USA

Or email:
bcd@degree.net

Do let us know of any mistakes or outdated information you find in this book; we will post corrections at *www.degree.net/updates/computerdegrees*.

Appendix C: For Information on Schools Not in This Book

There are four reasons why a school in which you might be interested is not described in this book:

1. It might be relevant, but we chose not to designate it one of the best schools.

2. It is not relevant for this book since it does not offer degrees entirely or mostly by home study.

3. It's new and we hadn't heard about it before this book went to press. (If so, write and tell us about it.)

4. It does not have recognized accreditation.

If you have questions about a school that is not described in this book, here is what we suggest, in the following order:

1. Check *Bears' Guide to Earning Degrees by Distance Learning*, which is a complete source for all distance-learning programs, and is published by Ten Speed Press. In it we list over 2500 schools that offer degrees by home study—good, bad, and otherwise. For more information, write to us at the address below, or visit our Web site at *www.degree.net*.

2. Look it up in one of the standard school directories that you can find in any public library or bookstore: Lovejoy's, Barron's, Peterson's, Patterson's, ARCO, and half a dozen others. These books describe virtually every traditional college and university in the United States and Canada.

3. Ask for the help of a reference librarian. Your tax dollars pay their salaries.

4. If you know the location of the school, even just the state, check with the relevant state education agency.

If none of the above approaches produce any useful information, then write to us and we will do what we can to help.

Enclose a self-addressed, stamped envelope.

If you want extensive advice or opinions on your personal situation, you will need to use the Degree Consulting Service described in Appendix D. Don't get too annoyed if we don't respond promptly. We do our best, but we get overwhelmed sometimes, and we travel a lot.

Please don't telephone.

Write to us at:

Best Computer Degrees
Degree.net
P.O. Box 7123
Berkeley, CA 94707

bcd@degree.net

Appendix D: For Personal Advice on Your Own Situation

If you would like advice and recommendations on your own specific situation, a personal counseling service offers this information, by mail only. John started this service in 1977 at the request of many readers. While he still remains a consultant, since 1981 the actual consulting and personal evaluations have been done by two colleagues of his, who are leading experts in the field of nontraditional education. For a modest consulting fee, these things are done:

1. You will get a long personal letter evaluating your situation, recommending the best degree programs for you (including part-time programs in your area, if relevant) and estimating how long it will take and what it will cost you to complete your degree(s).

2. You will get answers to any specific questions you may have with regard to programs you may now be considering, institutions you have already dealt with, or other relevant matters.

3. You will get detailed, up-to-the-minute information on institutions and degree programs, equivalency exams, sources of the correspondence courses you may need, career opportunities, resume writing, sources of financial aid, and other topics in the form of extensive prepared notes.

4. You will be entitled to telephone the service for a full year for unlimited follow-up counseling, to keep updated on new programs and other changes, and to otherwise use the service as your personal information resource.

If you are interested in this personal counseling, please write or call and you will be sent descriptive literature and a counseling questionnaire, without cost or obligation.

If, once you have these materials, you do want counseling, simply fill out the questionnaire and return it, with a letter and resume if you like, along with the fee. Your personal reply and counseling materials will be airmailed to you as quickly as possible.

For free information about this service, write, telephone, or email:

Degree Consulting Services
P.O. Box 3533
Santa Rosa, CA 95402
Phone: (707) 539 6466
Fax: (707) 538 3577
Email: degrees@sonic.net.
Web site: www.degreeconsult.com

Appendix E: Bending the Rules

One of the most common complaints or admonishments we hear from readers goes something like this: "You said thus-and-so, but when I inquired of the school, they told me such-and-such." It has happened (although rarely) that a school claims that a program we have written about does not exist. Sometimes a student achieves something (such as completing a certain degree entirely by correspondence) that we had been told by a high official of the school was impossible.

One of the open secrets in the world of higher education is that the rules are constantly being bent. But as with the Emperor's new clothes, no one dares to point and say what is really going on, especially in print.

Unfortunately, we cannot provide many specific examples of bent rules, naming names and all. This is for two good reasons:

1. Many situations where students profit from bent rules would disappear in an instant if anyone dared mention the situation publicly. There is, for instance, a major state university that is forbidden by its charter to grant degrees for correspondence study. But they regularly work out special arrangements for students who are carried on the books as residential students even though all work is done by mail. Indeed, some graduates have never set foot on campus. If this ever got out, the Board of Trustees, the relevant accrediting agency, and all the other universities in that state would probably have conniptions, and the practice would be suspended at once.

2. These kinds of things can change so rapidly, particularly with new personnel or new policies, that a listing of anomalies and curious practices would probably be obsolete before the ink dried.

Consider a few examples of the sort of thing that is going on in higher education every day, whether or not anyone will admit it, except perhaps behind closed doors or after several drinks:

- A friend of John's at a major university was unable to complete one required course for her doctorate before she had to leave for another state. This university does not offer correspondence courses, but she was able to convince a professor to enroll her in a regular course, which she would just happen never to visit in person.

- A man in graduate school needed to be enrolled in nine units of coursework each semester to keep his employer's tuition-assistance plan going. But his job was too demanding one year, and he was unable to do so. The school enrolled him in nine units of "independent study" for which no work was asked or required, and for which a "pass" grade was given.

- A woman at a large school needed to get a certain number of units before an inflexible time deadline. When it was clear she was not going to make it, a kindly professor turned in grades for her, and told her she could do the actual coursework later on.

- A major state university offers nonresident degrees for people living in that state only. When a reader wrote to John saying that he, living a thousand miles from that state, was able to complete his degree entirely by correspondence, we asked a contact at that school what was going on. "We will take students from anywhere in our correspondence degree program," she told us. "But for God's sake, don't print that in your book, or we'll be deluged with applicants."

Please use this information prudently. It will probably do no good to pound on a table and say, "What do you mean, I can't do this? John Bear says that rules don't mean anything, anyway." But when faced with a problem, it surely can do no harm to remember that there do exist many situations in which the rules have turned out to be far less rigid than the printed literature of a school would lead you to believe.

Subject Index

Accounting Information Systems
St. Mary-of-the-Woods College (B, SR)

Business Administration (IT-Focused)
Athabasca University (M, NR)
Auburn University (M, NR)
Bellevue University (M, NR)
Capella University (M, NR)
City University (M, NR)
Drexel University (M, NR)
Regent University (M, NR)
University of Phoenix Online (M, NR)

Business Information Systems
Bellevue University (B, NR)
Monash University (M, NR)
University of Phoenix Online (B, NR)
University of Southern Queensland
(M, NR)

Computational Linguistics
University of Kent at Canterbury
(M-D, SR)

Computational Physics
Murdoch University (B, NR)

**Computational Social Sciences
and Humanities**
University of Melbourne (M-D, NR)

Computer-Aided Design
University of Houston (B, NR)

Computer-Aided Language Learning
University of Melbourne (M-D, NR)

Computer Education
University of Melbourne (M-D, NR)

Computer Engineering
Auburn University (M, NR)
Excelsior College (B, NR)
Georgia Institute of Technology (M, NR)
Iowa State University (M, NR)
Mississippi State University (M, NR)
National Technological University
(M, NR)
Rensselaer Polytechnic Institute (M, NR)
Thomas Edison State College (B, NR)
University of Idaho (M, NR)
University of Massachusetts at Amherst
(M, NR)
University of Southern California (M, NR)
University of Southern Queensland
(M, NR)
University of Technology, Sydney (D, NR)
University of Texas (M, NR)
University of Wisconsin at Madison
(M, NR)

Computer Game Design
University of Abertay Dundee
(M, NR)

Computer Graphics and Imaging Science
Rochester Institute of Technology
(B-M, NR)
St. Mary-of-the-Woods College (B, SR)
University of Bradford (M-D, SR)

Computer Information Systems
Athabasca University (B-M, NR)
Caldwell College (B, SR)
Central Queensland University (M, NR)
Champlain College (B, NR)
Charter Oak State College (B, NR)
City University (B-M, NR)
Columbia Union College (B, SR)
Drexel University (M, NR)
Edith Cowan University (B, NR)
Excelsior College (B, NR)
National Technological University
(M, NR)
New Jersey Institute of Technology
(B, NR)
Nova Southeastern University
(M, NR; D, SR)
Park University (B, NR)
Regis University (M, NR)
St. Mary-of-the-Woods College (B, SR)
Southwest Missouri State University
(M, NR)
Strayer University (B-M, NR)
University of Denver (M, NR)
University of London (B, NR; M-D, SR)
University of Maryland (B-M, NR)
University of Massachusetts at Lowell
(A-B, NR)
University of Melbourne (M-D, NR)
University of Phoenix Online (B-M, NR)
University of South Africa (B-M, NR)
University of Southern Queensland
(M, NR)
University of Tasmania (M-D, SR)
University of Technology, Sydney (D, NR)

Computer-Mediated Communication
Regent University (M, NR)

Computer Programming
See **Software Engineering**

Computer Science
Atlantic Union College (B, SR)
Ball State University (M, SR)
California State University—Chico
(B-M, NR)
Charter Oak State College (B, NR)

B = Bachelor's • M = Master's • D = Doctorate • NR = Nonresident • SR = Short Residency

151

Computer Science (continued)
Colorado State University (M, NR)
Columbus State University (M, NR)
Florida State University (B, NR)
Franklin University (B, NR)
Lakeland College (B, NR)
Mercy College (B, NR)
Mississippi State University (M, NR)
Murdoch University (B, NR)
National Technological University (M, NR)
New Jersey Institute of Technology (B, NR)
Nova Southeastern University (M, NR; D, SR)
Rensselaer Polytechnic Institute (M, NR)
Southern Methodist University (M, NR)
Southwestern Adventist University (B, SR)
Thomas Edison State College (B, NR)
University of Colorado at Boulder (M, NR)
University of Houston (M, NR)
University of Idaho (M, NR)
University of Illinois at Urbana-Champaign (M, NR)
University of Kent at Canterbury (M-D, SR)
University of Maryland (B, NR)
University of Massachusetts at Amherst (M, NR)
University of New England (M-D, NR)
University of South Africa (B-M-D, NR)
University of Southern California (M, NR)
University of Technology (D, NR)
University of Texas (M, NR)
University of Wales—Aberystwyth (M-D, SR)

Computing
Central Queensland University (D, NR)
Monash University (B, NR)
Rochester Institute of Technology (B, NR)
South Bank University (M-D, SR)
United States Open University (B-M, NR)
University of Bradford (M-D, SR)
University of London (B, NR; M-D, SR)
University of Luton (M-D, SR)
University of Southern Queensland (M, NR)
University of Tasmania (M-D, SR)
University of Teesside (M-D, SR)

Data Mining and Knowledge Discovery
University of Glasgow (M, NR)

Educational Technology (IT-Focused)
Lesley University (M, NR)
Marlboro College (M, SR)
Nova Southeastern University (M, NR; D, SR)
University of Southern Queensland (M, NR)

Electronic Commerce and Internet Strategy
Bellevue University (B, NR)
Capella University (M, NR; D, SR)
Capitol College (M, NR)
City University (B, NR)
Marlboro College (M, SR)
Monash University (B, NR)
National University (M, NR)
Rochester Institute of Technology (B, NR)
University of Maryland (M, NR)
University of Southern Queensland (M, NR)

Environmental Information Technology
Charles Sturt University (D, NR)

Geographic Information Systems
South Bank University (M-D, SR)
University of Southern Queensland (M, NR)

Health Information Systems
Central Queensland University (M, NR)
University of Southern Queensland (M, NR)

Individualized (can be IT-Focused)
Charter Oak State College (B, NR)
Empire State College (B, NR)
Judson College (B, NR)
Lesley University (M, NR)
Norwich University (B-M, SR)
Oklahoma City University (B, SR)
Rochester Institute of Technology (M, NR)
St. Mary-of-the-Woods College (B, SR)
Skidmore College (B, SR)
Southwestern Adventist University (B, SR)
Union Institute (B-D, SR)
University of Wisconsin at Superior (B, NR)

Industrial Technology (IT-Focused)
East Carolina University (M, NR)

Informatics
Central Queensland University (B, NR)
University of South Africa (B, NR)

Information Science (IT-Focused)
Charles Sturt University (D, NR)
Drexel University (M, NR)
Edith Cowan University (M, NR)
Florida State University (B-M, NR)
Syracuse University (M, SR)
University of South Australia (B, NR)
University of Technology, Sydney (D, NR)
University of Tennessee at Knoxville (M, SR)

Information Technology
Capella University (B)
Central Queensland University (B, NR)
Charles Sturt University (B-M-D, NR)
Harvard University (M, SR)
ISIM University (M, NR)
Monash University (M, NR)
Rensselaer Polytechnic Institute (M, NR)
Rochester Institute of Technology (M, NR)
United States Open University (B, NR)
University of Abertay Dundee (M, NR)
University of Maryland (M, NR)
University of Southern Queensland (B-M, NR)

Information Technology Law
University of Strathclyde (M, NR)

Information Technology Management
Capella University (M, NR; D, SR)
Capitol College (M, NR)
Curtin University of Technology (M, NR)
Franklin University (B, NR)
ISIM University (M, NR)
Keller Graduate School of Management (M, NR)
Monash University (M, NR)
National Technological University (M, NR)
Syracuse University (M, SR)
University of Maryland (B-M, NR)
University of Oregon (M, NR)
University of Southern Queensland (B, NR)
Upper Iowa University (B, NR)
See also **Business Administration (IT-Focused)**

B = Bachelor's • M = Master's • D = Doctorate • NR = Nonresident • SR = Short Residency

Internet Engineering and Applications
Capitol College (B, NR)
Marlboro College (M, SR)
St. Mary-of-the-Woods College
(B, SR)

Internet Studies
Curtin University of Technology
(M-D, NR)

Management Information Systems
Bellevue University (B, NR)
Deakin University (M, NR)
Franklin University (B, NR)
Judson College (B, NR)
Nova Southeastern University
(M, NR)
University of Illinois at Springfield
(M, NR)

MBA (IT-Focused)
See **Business Administration
(IT-Focused)**

Microelectronics
Rochester Institute of Technology
(M, NR)
University of Southern California
(M, NR)

Multimedia
Central Queensland University
(B, NR)
Monash University (B-M, NR)
University of Bradford (M-D, SR)
University of Melbourne (M-D, NR)
University of Technology, Sydney
(D, NR)
University of Teesside (M-D, SR)

Networking
Monash University (M, NR)
Strayer University (B, NR)
Syracuse University (M, SR)

Online Education
Capella University (M, NR; D, SR)
Marlboro College (M, SR)
University of Southern Queensland
(M, NR)

Robotics
University of Bradford (M-D, SR)

Software Applications
Capitol College (B, NR)
Excelsior College (A, NR)

Software Engineering
Auburn University (M, NR)
Carnegie Mellon University (M, NR)
Champlain College (A, NR)
Florida State University (B, NR)
Kansas State University (M, NR)
National Technological University
(M, NR)
Naval Postgraduate School (M, NR)
Rochester Institute of Technology
(M, NR)
Southern Methodist University
(M, NR)
Texas Tech University (M, NR)
University of Maryland (M, NR)
University of Melbourne (M-D, NR)

Spatial Information Systems
Charles Sturt University (B, NR)

Telecommunications
Capella University (M, NR; D, SR)
Capitol College (M, NR)
Champlain College (A, NR)
Golden Gate University (M, NR)
Keller Graduate School of
Management (M, NR)
Rochester Institute of Technology
(B, NR)
St. Mary-of-the-Woods College
(B, SR)
Southern Methodist University
(M, NR)
Stanford University (M, NR)
Syracuse University (M, SR)
University of Colorado at Boulder
(M, NR)
University of Denver (M, NR)
University of Maryland (M, NR)
University of South Australia
(B-M, NR)
University of Technology, Sydney
(D, NR)

Web Site Administration
Champlain College (B, NR)
University of Southern Queensland
(B, NR)

B = Bachelor's • M = Master's • D = Doctorate • NR = Nonresident • SR = Short Residency